FRANNI & THE DUKE

ANNE E. JOHNSON

Mechanicsburg, PA USA

Published by Sunbury Press, Inc.
105 South Market Street
Mechanicsburg, Pennsylvania 17055

www.sunburypress.com

ISBN: 978-1-62006-703-1 (Trade Paperback)
ISBN: 978-1-62006-704-8 (Mobipocket)

Library of Congress Control Number: 2016943450

FIRST SUNBURY PRESS EDITION: July 2016

Product of the United States of America
0 1 1 2 3 5 8 13 21 34 55

Set in Bookman Old Style
Designed by Crystal Devine
Cover by Amber Rendon
Edited by Allyson Gard

Continue the Enlightenment!

CHAPTER 1

Thursday, May 8, 1608

"I'm hungry," said Franni. She ached all over from hours of walking down rocky roads in the Northern Italian countryside. "Please, can we get some food, Alli?" She shivered in the chilly spring drizzle.

Franni's older sister, Alessandra, walked in front as usual. She looked back and smiled weakly. "I know you're hungry, Franni. I am, too." Alli's eyes were glassy in her drawn face. "We're almost to Mantua. That's a big city with lots of rich people. I'm sure someone will take pity on us there."

Although Franni doubted it, she nodded. A day and a half ago, they'd run away from their stepfather in Verona. They'd left in the middle of the night, carrying only a satchel of clothes each, and one loaf of bread between them. The last town they'd been through hadn't shown them much pity. When they'd taken a drink at the central fountain, a soldier had chased them right out of town.

"I'm so tired." She hardly had the strength to get any sound out. There was no way Franni could take another step, so she sat down right there in the road.

Alli grabbed Franni's elbow and yanked. "Come *on.* We've got to get to Mantua before the sun goes down." A slender, delicate creature of seventeen, Alli was no match for Franni when the younger girl felt stubborn. Franni willed herself to weigh as much as the elephant her real father once saw in Algiers. He'd said it was the size of twenty men. Closing her eyes, Franni glued herself to the paving stones, thinking heavy thoughts.

"A cart!" Alli let go of Franni's arm and stood up, waving.

Franni's heavy mood turned to dandelion seeds and floated away. "A cart?" She craned to see the black horse drawing a workman's cart slowly along the road toward them. "Do you think he'll give us a ride?"

"He has to," said Alli. It sounded like a prayer. "He just has to."

We're saved! thought Franni. But when the cart pulled near enough that they could smell the tang of horse sweat, she changed her mind. "He's an undertaker," she whispered. "Look at the white marble slabs he's dragging in that cart. It would be bad luck to ride with him." She backed off the road and pulled her embroidered scarf over her head and face.

To Franni's distress, Alli stepped into the middle of the road and waved her arms wider. If only their mother could see them now, two noble girls, behaving like beggars. Surely Mama *could* see them as she looked down from Heaven. She probably also saw how their stepfather treated the girls after their mother died. Franni was sure Mama up in Heaven approved of how she and Alli had sneaked out of the gates of Verona one night to find a happier life.

"Whoa!" said the cart driver, pulling back on the horse's reins. "What is it, child? Why are you in the road? Do you need help?"

He didn't shout insults at them, like every other driver had done so far. Impressed at this man's kindness, Franni pulled back her scarf to look at him more closely. He was old, with gray hair poking out from his floppy leather hat. He had no teeth, and showed the hunched bearing of a servant.

"Old man," said Alli, "we need a ride to Mantua." She spoke proudly, like the merchant's daughter that she was.

Franni stepped forward and spoke flatly. "Are you an undertaker?"

"Franni!" her sister scolded.

But she had to know before she'd climb into that cart, no matter how desperately she wanted to rest her feet. She pointed at the marble slabs tied into his cart. "Will those be used for gravestones?"

The old man laughed. "You're a smart one, aren't you?" He winked at Franni and gave Alli a humble bow of his head. "I'm just carrying these slabs to the crew building the new Exhibition Gallery, across from the Cortina della Cavallerizza."

Franni furrowed her brow at the word *Cavallerizza.* "The court of the horsewoman? Why would a horsewoman have her own court? And what's an Exhibition?"

"Franni! You're being annoying," her sister scolded again. Alli was always worried about correct behavior.

"I'm just asking him a question. You don't mind, do you, Signore?"

The man grinned and reached out his hand. "I don't mind talking, but I can't stay here. Let's all talk about marble and Mantua on the way. Hop in, girls."

Still nimble despite being so tired, Franni climbed up onto the driver's bench. The man laughed. "Look at you climb, little girl! You go in the back. Your sister's a grown lady, so she shall sit up front."

"I'm not a little girl!" Franni protested. "I'm twelve years old!" But she knew she'd never win this fight. At seventeen, Alli was a grown-up, so she got to make decisions. But Franni tried one more argument. "What if I get squashed by the stone?"

The driver laughed again, a habit that was starting to annoy Franni. "It took six men just to load on that one piece. This road is flat and fairly smooth. That marble's not going anywhere. Now, mind *you* don't harm *it,* or I'll lose my job."

Wondering what she could do to damage a huge slab of rock, Franni crawled into the back and used her bag of clothes to soften a pointy marble corner. It seemed to her that she would never be comfortable again.

With a flick of the reins, the driver coaxed his horse to move. It didn't seem pleased at the weight of its load, judging by how its flanks bulged with each slow step. But the driver didn't seem to notice. He chattered as if he were a prince on holiday.

"I know the little girl is called Franni. You've said her name, enough. And you, my dear?" he asked Alli. She just looked away.

"Her name is Alessandra," Franni volunteered. "Alli for short."

"What a delightful name! And you may call me Carlo."

"Nice to meet you, Carlo," said Franni energetically. She was always happy to get to know new people. Her sister, on the other hand, didn't trust anyone who wasn't a handsome young man. Alli just nodded.

But if Carlo felt slighted, he didn't show it. "And what brings you two lovely girls to be wandering along this road all on your own? The Via Verona is no place for the likes of you."

Franni, who always preferred to tell the truth when possible, got ready to say, "We're running away from our crazy stepfather in Verona." But Alli answered too quickly.

"Our uncle lives in Mantua. We wanted to surprise him with a visit."

A soft groan escaped from Franni. They had no uncle in Mantua. Alli seemed to love to build complicated lies.

"Your uncle. Is that a fact, now?" said the driver. When he turned his head, Franni could see the sympathetic glimmer in his eye. He didn't believe Alli's story, but Franni knew better than to interfere. "And what might your uncle's name be?"

"Oh, you wouldn't know him," said Alli, "because he's just a merchant."

And because he doesn't exist, thought Franni.

"Nonsense, my dear." The old man gave a hearty laugh, which was echoed by a whinny from his horse. "I know hundreds of merchants. I deliver supplies to them as my daily work. What sort of business is your uncle in?"

Franni could tell from Alli's hunched shoulders that she was trying to think up something believable. *This is what comes of lying,* Franni thought for the thousandth time. But most people never seemed to learn that.

"He's a baker," Alli finally said, after too long a pause.

"Well, then, I'm sure I know him. I bring flour into town all the time. Right along this route, in fact. Where's his bakehouse?"

Alli was silent, clearly out of ideas. When she sniffled a little, Franni felt sorry for her, and reached her hand up to stroke her sister's back. Apparently Carlo felt sorry for her, too, because he changed the subject. "This narrow road between these lakes is called the Via dei mulini."

"The Mill Road?" sighed Alli, looking around. "Oh, my, what large lakes! They stretch on and on! Look, Franni!"

The driver pointed to their right. "That one's called Upper Lake." He pointed the other way. "That's Middle Lake."

"Those are very boring names for lakes," Franni complained.

"There's also a Lower Lake. I like their names," said Carlo. "They're very straightforward." He turned back and winked. "Like you."

Franni couldn't help but grin. "Maybe they're not such bad names, after all."

"They were dug centuries ago, by a prince trying to protect the city of Mantua. And then there's the big natural lake, Lake Pajolo, straight across from here, below the swampland. Its water is so high sometimes, the roads flood."

Franni pulled herself up to her knees excitedly. "Papa said Venice is like that, too."

"Venice has much more water than Mantua," said the driver. Then he turned to look at Franni. "Does your Papa know where you are?"

Knowing their father was watching them from Heaven, right next to their mother, Franni answered truthfully. "Yes."

"Hmm." He sounded like he wasn't convinced. But he wasn't the sort to dwell on things too long, it seemed. In a moment he was distracted by a coach coming from the other direction. The two horses pulling it wore purple and gold bridles and headdresses. The coach itself was white, with golden sculpted flowers all over it. When Carlo doffed his floppy hat in greeting, the driver of the coach lifted his nose and looked at the sky.

"God save Our Gracious Duke!" Carlo cried happily as the fancy coach rolled past. He looked back, perhaps to see if they were out of earshot, then whispered to the girls. "Duke Vincenzo Gonzaga likes pretty things, as you can see."

"Was that the Duke?" Alli asked. Suddenly she was all smiles and bright eyes.

"The Duke himself would never travel with only a single coach. He'd have a full retinue."

Alli sighed. "How fascinating! Do you know him?"

Carlo had a big, belly-shaking laugh as he snapped the reins and got his horse moving again. "Good Heavens, child. Do I look like I would know a duke?"

"Alli wants to find a duke or a prince and marry him," Franni blurted out. "She says there are lots of such people in Mantua, and it's only a matter of time before we meet one."

"Franni!" Alli crossed her arms and huffed.

"Well, then, we're going down the right street," said Carlo with a big laugh. "The Duke of Mantua himself lives there just beyond the city gate."

"Really?" asked Alli, craning to see. Suddenly she didn't seem angry at Franni, just excited. "Do you think we'll get a chance to see him?"

Franni rolled her eyes. The last thing she cared about was looking at dukes. "Maybe we should worry about where we're going to sleep tonight. And where we'll get some dinner." Just as she said that, she remembered Alli's tall tale about having an uncle in Mantua. "Oops." She tried to jump back into the lie. "I mean, we should find out if Uncle is at home." She barely had the nerve to look up at Alli's glowering face.

The cart slowed to a stop as they approached the entrance gate, and suddenly they were surrounded by soldiers. This was a relief for Franni. The handsome guards distracted her sister from strangling her. Alli straightened up in her seat and fidgeted with her bonnet. Although Franni was behind her, she was sure Alli was batting her eyelids at the black-haired guard in the gold-embroidered uniform. The guard checked Carlo's papers and favored Alli with a lopsided grin. He paid no attention to Franni. That suited her just fine.

And then they saw the palace, the Palazzo Ducale. Its reddish brick walls were decorated with hundreds of pointed archways. Its majestic entranceway was lined with perfectly trimmed bushes and flowers. Alli, of course, was practically swooning. Franni was disappointed.

"I thought it would be made of gold and marble."

Carlo shook his head. "I've made some deliveries here. All the gold and marble is inside. And paintings and vases and all kinds of crazy, expensive things. The Duke is nuts for art. And the Palazzo is much bigger than it looks. It's practically a small city. I'll show you. We'll ride all the way around it."

They clomped along forever. With each turn, the red brick and pointed arches showed up for another block. It really was like a separate, walled town, right there in the middle of Mantua.

"One day," Alli said with a wobbly voice, "one day I'll be invited to enter that Palazzo."

Franni sighed. Carlo glanced back at her and winked. She liked this fellow. He understood her. And he said the perfect thing. "Your uncle's probably not home, eh? I'll show you someplace safe you can stay for the night."

Carlo is a kind man, thought Franni, glancing at the sky. *Mama and Papa must have guided him to us.* This thought gave her hope. Perhaps Mantua would be a city of good fortune for them after all.

CHAPTER 2

THE CART WENDED THROUGH THE streets of Mantua until there was no sign of all those elegant buildings and lawns. Carlo pulled up in front of a shack where a woman was waving at them.

"That's Bianca," said Carlo as they pulled up in front of her shack of a house. "She's a washerwoman. Good, honest work."

Bianca had the broadest shoulders Franni had ever seen. She could have snapped Franni in two like a bread stick. When Bianca opened her arms to embrace Carlo, Franni worried he would be crushed. But he just laughed and let himself be covered in kisses.

"Remember, Bianca, I have a wife!" he said, and she put her head back and whooped with delight. Then, a bit more seriously, he said, "These two just arrived in Mantua. Need a place to stay until their, er, *uncle* comes back into town." Franni could see him wink.

Bianca let Carlo loose and turned her attention to the cart. She headed for Alli first. Alli pulled away, and Franni could barely watch. "Come on now, pretty one," Bianca cooed with a voice that would set a whole flock of birds flapping from their tree branches. "I won't bite you, dear."

"Tough as a sergeant on the outside, our Bianca may be. But she's a plum cake on the inside, she is," Carlo assured them, reaching over the side of the cart to pat Franni's head. "Come along, children. Come inside."

Franni, tired of being wedged in with the marble, climbed out eagerly and dropped onto the wet ground. Her feet sank into the mud past her ankles. "Oh."

"This street never seems to dry all spring long," said Bianca, shaking her head and gesturing around her run-down block. "All those fancy buildings and parks and entertainments, but not one silver scudo coin to pave our streets. You can be sure the Duke . . ."

"Shhh!" warned Carlo, looking around frantically. "Don't want the wrong ears to hear that sort of talk." Loudly, and to no one in particular, he said, "Long live our Duke. Mighty Vincenzo Gonzaga, pride of Mantua."

Bianca just snickered and began to drag Alli from the cart. "My shoes!" Alli cried. But it was too late.

Franni, who usually loved to tease her sister for being so vain, felt awful for her. She slopped over to Bianca and shouted, her fists balled at her sides. "You didn't have to pull her out. You could've helped her."

"I'm not your servant, child," Bianca said, "and I'll thank you to remember I'm giving you a dry place to sleep, and you no kin of mine." She waddled into her wooden shack.

To Franni's amazement, Carlo seemed to think this was a perfectly normal way for Bianca to treat guests. "Okay, I'll leave you to it, then," he said, climbing back into the driver's seat. "I've got to make these deliveries."

Franni whispered urgently, "We can't stay here! Please let us come with you, Carlo!"

Carlo sighed. "I can't show up at my appointments with two road-weary young girls. And you two need a place to stay." He looked at Franni sharply. "Unless you think your uncle's back by now?"

There was nothing for Franni to say. She'd had such hope in Carlo, but clearly there were no adults she could trust. None but her own true parents, and they were gone. She took the elbow of her blubbering sister and led her toward Bianca's house.

"Psst!"

Franni turned to see what Carlo wanted.

"If you have any talents or skills," he said, "you should spend the day tomorrow in the area near the Duke's Palazzo. You never know who might be passing by and hear you sawing out a tune on your violin or tooting on your flute."

With that, he slapped the reins against the back of his tired horse. The cart wheels made a sucking sound as they pulled away from the muddy curb.

"We don't even have a violin," Franni said quietly, knowing he couldn't hear. "Or a flute."

"What did you say?" Alli asked. Her eyes were red.

"A violin. We don't have a violin. We can't play music for anybody."

"Franni, that's it!" Alli whispered. "We'll spend the night here and leave at first light tomorrow."

Bianca's rough voice cut all the way across the house. "Hey, new girls! Fetch the laundry from the back yard!"

Franni had no idea what Alli's plan was, but she liked it anyway. As the daughters of a successful merchant, they were not used to being ordered around or doing anyone else's laundry. Back home, they'd had servants of their own. Anything would be better than this, it seemed to Franni. She trudged out back, following Alli, and fought to fold the half-frozen bedsheets with numb fingers. This was no life for her.

* * *

"Wake up!" Franni felt herself jostled out of a troubled sleep. The cold morning air made her cough. "Shh!" hissed Alli. "We have to go."

Now running away from this stinky old house didn't seem like such a great idea. At least it was a bed and a roof over their head. They'd been served a stew last night and would probably get bread this morning. "Where are we going?" Franni asked nervously.

Her fingers to her lips, Alli pulled Franni from the mattress. "Come on!"

Half asleep, Franni ran through the early morning streets, Alli dragging her by the hand. She had no idea where they were, but she had to trust her sister. All Franni wanted to do was curl up by the side of the road and go back to sleep.

"Watch out!" A cart with two horses clattered past them just as Alli heaved Franni out of the way.

The jolt woke Franni up. "This is ridiculous. What's going on?" she demanded. "We had a place to stay in a strange city. What are you doing to us?"

"I'm taking your friend's suggestion."

"What friend? What suggestion?"

"That Carlo fellow."

"He's not my friend."

Ignoring her protest, Alli pointed several blocks down the road. "See those fancy marble buildings?"

"Yeah. So?"

"We're going to spend the day in that rich neighborhood. By the Duke's Palazzo."

Franni groaned. "Enough with the Duke!"

"No, listen. Your friend Carlo was right. I'll sing."

"Sing?"

"I'm a good singer, right?"

In truth, Alli had the sweetest voice Franni had ever heard. But she was also Franni's sister. "You sing pretty well."

"Okay, so I'll sing, and people will give us money." As she said this, Alli took off down the road at a brisk pace.

Struggling to keep up, Franni asked, "Why will they give us money?"

"Because you'll pass a hat, and they'll drop florins and scudi into it. Come on!" Alli grabbed Franni's hand again and sped up to nearly a run.

It was all Franni could do to flop along behind. Her feet were blistered after their long trek from Verona, and every time her boot hit the paving stones she winced. "Slow down," she pleaded. But Alli paid no attention.

Finally they stopped in an alcove made of carved marble. In the center of it was a bronze sculpture of a man. Franni flicked the frost off the dedication plate and read it aloud. "Frederico II, House of Gonzaga, Duke of Mantua." She turned to her sister, who was rubbing her throat with her scarf. "Was that the man in that fancy carriage yesterday? And what are you doing to your neck?"

"The current duke is named Vincenzo," said Alli, who had an amazing memory for things like that. "And I'm warming my throat so I can sing in this chilly air."

"I think you might be crazy." Franni slumped onto a marble edge jutting out from the alcove. "And I guess that makes me crazy too, for tagging along."

But Alli ignored her. Folding her hands primly, she cleared her throat and began to sing in an angelic voice:

Praise the savior of Zion,
Praise the leader and shepherd
With hymns and songs.

A few people walked by, huddled against the cold. Most didn't even look at Alli. But worse were those who glanced up with a pity in their eyes that made Franni want to scream. Alli continued:

Let our praise be full, let it resonate,
Let it be joyous, let it be beautiful.

Their mother used to sing that *lauda*. Hearing it crushed Franni's heart. There was nothing she could do to keep from crying. Alli stopped singing and rubbed her hand against Franni's back, but Franni pulled away. She didn't want to be comforted. She would never be happy again. She just knew it. Might as well grow used to this feeling of misery that seemed to sit in her bones.

"Come on, Franni, it'll be all right." Alli cooed in a melodious voice that also reminded Franni of their mother, but in a nicer way. Just having her sister nearby comforted her, in spite of herself. "Want to sing the *Nano-noe*?"

Franni loved that lullaby, but she ran both palms over her teary cheeks and shook her head. "You know how terrible my voice is," she choked between sobs. "The guards will run us out of town if I sing."

With a little laugh, Alli kissed Franni's forehead. "Silly-nilly. You just sit there, then. You're shivering. Take my shawl." Alli unwrapped the cloth from her shoulders. Franni could see Alli's body tense in the wind, but she let Alli arrange the shawl on top of her own.

"Thanks," she whispered.

"Okay, but now you need to try to look a little happier." Alli put her cold hands on Franni's cheeks. "You'll never feel happy if you don't show Heaven your happy face. That's how they know how you'd like to feel, remember?"

Franni did remember. That was something their father used to say. And it always brought a smile though her tears. It worked this morning, too, but the smile was more painful to form than in the past. Still, it gave her strength, as it always did.

"Maybe I should forget the religious songs," Alli said. "How about a love song?"

Franni decided there must be some way she could help. "Hold on. I'll find you an audience," she declared, heading off down the block.

She heard Alli shout, "Come back, Franni," but when an idea took hold of Franni, nothing would stop her. She ran down the street toward a man who was shuffling along, carrying a case. Franni's extended family included many musicians, so she knew a violin case when she saw one.

"Hey!" she shouted, startling him from a private reverie. "Looks like you like music!" The puzzled look on his face made her remember her manners. She made an awkward curtsy. "I beg your pardon, sir," she tried again. "My sister has a lovely voice. She'll sing you a song for a florin."

At first the man said nothing. He was tall and thin, and he looked tired. Not just bleary because it was morning, but weary from daily life. Franni started to worry that he wouldn't have a florin to spare. That was a lot to charge for one song that her sister would normally sing for free while washing her hair. "You only have to pay fifty denari," Franni bargained desperately.

The man gave her a gentle, encouraging smile. "Now, now," he said, "don't sell your sister short. Let me hear her, and I'll decide the price for the song. But it won't be lower than fifty denari."

Afraid he'd change his mind, Franni snatched the man's free hand and yanked him toward the statue of the duke, where Alli stood with her hands on her head and her eyes wide in horror. "Franni! Leave that poor man alone!"

"He's a musician," Franni announced. "He wants to hear something modern. Something in the latest style."

"Do I?" asked the man, tipping his hat to Alli. "I'd be delighted to hear whatever you'd care to sing, Signorina."

Rubbing her hands nervously, Alli cleared her throat several times before she said, "This is by Luca Marenzio, in the latest style."

I cry because love burns and eats my heart
with the unburned rage of a new flame.

"Well, *that's* depressing," Franni interrupted, kicking at the marble base of the statue. "I'm sure sir would like something happier."

"No, no!" said the violinist. "Do go on."

A smile flashed across Alli's face, but then she seemed to force it into a frown. Franni could tell she was acting to match the sad song.

I sigh because I'm an unlucky lover
Who can't enjoy the green and blossoming May.
I feel pain because two beautiful eyes
Don't notice my tears in their shining gaze.
Maybe, out of pity, those eyes will end
My sorrow, sighs, and bitter weeping.

When Alli fell silent, the man didn't respond. He just stood there. Franni was ready to kick him in the shins if it would loosen a coin from his fist. But then his face relaxed into a huge smile and he reached into his pocket. "I'll give you a florin if you like, but I'd rather give you something even better. You should come with me."

Alli gasped. "Sir, we're virtuous girls!"

Bowing so deeply that his violin case scraped the paving stones, the man said, "Ah, please forgive me. I never imagined you were anything but an angel with a voice like that. I only meant that I know someone who would hire you to sing. Indoors, where it's warm!"

Franni crossed her arms and glared at him. The man bowed again. "Please allow me to introduce myself. I am Giuseppe Ruffo. As you see, I play the violin."

"I'm not interested in singing a duet with you, sir," said Alli with a sneer.

"Signorina, I sincerely apologize if I have offended you. Please let me be clear. I play the violin at the Palazzo Ducale."

Alli's sneer turned into a beaming smile. "You actually play for the Duke of Mantua, Signore Ruffo?"

"That's correct. What is your name, my dear?"

"I'm Alessandra Ategnati. And this is my little sister, Francesca."

"Ategnati, eh? You come from a musical family," the violinist said. "Now I'm even more certain that the Duke may have use for a talented singer such as yourself."

"Oh, Franni," sighed Alli, clutching her sister's arm, "I'm going to the Palazzo to sing!"

CHAPTER 3

GIUSEPPE RUFFO HAD LONG LEGS. It was tough work for Franni to keep up with him. But Alli seemed to be floating over the paving stones. "Will I sing for the Duke himself?" she asked the violinist.

"No. For his musical director, his *maestro di capella.* Claudio Monteverdi."

"I've heard of him!" Alli gushed.

No, you haven't, Franni thought crossly.

"Just one thing," said the violinist to Alli. "When you meet Maestro Monteverdi, don't say that Marenzio is the latest style. He'll throw you out on the street."

"But Marenzio is very famous," Alli argued.

"True, but Monteverdi is sure that he himself is the latest, best style. And he is very fond of his own talents." Guiseppe grinned. "But you didn't hear that from me."

Franni was curious. "What will Alli be singing?"

"It doesn't matter," Alli said quickly. "I can sing anything."

They were passing by a castle. Beyond that was a huge garden with an iron fence twice Franni's height.

"Maestro Monteverdi has written a tragic musical show called *Arianna.* It will be part of the wedding festivities."

Alli stopped short. "Wedding?" she panted. "The Duke his getting married?"

Giuseppe laughed. "No, he's already married. It's his nephew. The Duke has commissioned all manner of entertainments, to last an entire week at the end of May."

It was Franni's turn to stop. "But it's already May. Shouldn't they be rehearsing by now?"

Shaking his head sadly, Giuseppe said, "Indeed, they've been rehearsing for many weeks. But there was a smallpox outbreak. We lost several singers and instrumentalists. Even the lead soprano, who was supposed to sing the role of Arianna herself, has died." He turned to Alli. "That's why I thought there may be a place for you."

"Oh!" Alli's exclaimed.

"I'm sure Giuseppe doesn't mean you'll get the lead part," Franni warned.

"That's true, I'm afraid," Giuseppe said. "But we could use some more women singing in the chorus." He looked back at Franni. "How about you? Can you sing?"

It was Alli who answered, "Definitely not."

"Never mind," laughed the violinist. "Tag along, and at least we'll get you some lunch."

That sounded fine to Franni. They'd passed by the wide gardens and now found themselves next to a construction site where hundreds of men were working to raise a gigantic wooden building. Franni was about to ask about it, but Alli cried out, "It's the Palazzo!" They could see the Duke of Mantua's dwelling a few streets down. Alli lifted her skirts slightly and hurried forward. Even long-legged Giuseppe seemed to struggle to keep up.

Franni fell behind. She was by herself when she noticed the strange-looking man. He had remarkably long arms. He was staring hard at the construction site. As Franni passed, the man turned and glared at her. She saw that his eyes were crooked in his skull, not evenly spaced on either side of his nose. Franni looked away, her pulse racing, and put all her effort into catching up to Alli and Giuseppe. When she did, she glanced back quickly. But the strange man was gone.

Giuseppe led them into a walkway shielded by the signature pointed arches, Alli froze again. "I'm not sure I'm ready to go into the Palazzo," she announced.

"But this is exactly what you wanted!" Franni wasn't feeling very safe after seeing that scary man at the construction site. "Let's just go inside." She liked the thought of the hundreds of guards that must be in the Palazzo, protecting the Duke. "What are we waiting for?"

"I think she's just nervous," Giuseppe chuckled. "Any singer would be. Come on, my dear. We'll get you some breakfast, let you wash your face, then take you to see Maestro Monteverdi."

Alli pinched her cheeks to bring color to them, straightened the kerchief on her hair, and dusted off her clothing with frantic motions.

"You look *fine*," groaned Franni. "Come *on*." She pulled Alli by the hand.

Carlo, the cart driver, had been right. The inside of the Palazzo was much more beautiful than the outside. Every surface was polished marble. Franni had no idea marble came in so many different colors and patterns. A golden maze decorated the ceiling.

Giuseppe must have noticed her face. "And this is just the servants' wing! Go in that door to your right, and you'll find something to eat."

Forgetting her manners completely, Franni hiked up her skirt and jogged on ahead of their guide, turning into the doorway he'd indicated. She expected to see some loaves of bread on a table. Now it was her turn to say, "Oh!"

Yes, there was bread. Five or six types of bread. And rolls. And cakes. And sausages. And cheeses. And fruits. In the center of the table sad a big, weird, ugly, prickly thing with huge green sprouts growing from its center. Franni couldn't take her eyes off the monster. It made her afraid to touch the food near it, as if it might reach out and scratch her hand.

"That is called a *pineapple*," Giuseppe explained. "Apparently you eat them, although I don't see how. The Duke has them imported from across the Atlantic Ocean." He lowered his voice to a whisper. "If it's exotic and expensive, His Highness wants it."

Someone behind them cackled with laughter. Franni spun to see a stately man with a strong jaw. He was dressed in a magnificent burgundy velvet tunic. "Who've we got here, Giuseppe?" He looked Franni up and down.

"Good morning, Signore Striggio. These are Alessandra and Francesca. The older one sings," Giuseppe explained. "I thought she might do for *Arianna.*" He handed a huge hunk of bread to Franni. "The younger one's just hungry." Franni wasn't pleased to be discussed in this way, but no power on Earth could have kept that slice of bread out of her mouth.

"Very well." The old man's missing teeth caused him to whistle when he spoke. "We mustn't keep the maestro waiting. Follow me."

He turned and left. Franni and Alli looked at each other.

"Well, let's go," sighed Giuseppe. "Signore Striggio is the director of *Arianna*, so we must do as he says." Giuseppe grabbed his violin case and left the room. Alli followed after him with short, awkward steps, as if she weren't very practiced at walking. Franni, grabbing two little cakes and a bunch of grapes, said a silent farewell to the stunning breakfast banquet and plodded after her sister.

They wandered through more hallways than Franni could keep track of. She stuffed her face as she walked, and at one point dropped a corner of a cake onto the pristine marble floor. Glancing around, she kicked it to the side, hoping nobody had seen. But someone had. A slender, delicate gray dog came prancing out of nowhere, lapped up the cake, and trot down the hallway. Its claws clattered on the marble floors.

When Franni turned around again, her sister and Giuseppe were gone. The beautifully carved marble walls and ceilings seemed ominous now, and the Palazzo felt so lonely that Franni's chest ached. "Alli?" She tiptoed forward, the taps of her boot soles echoing in the empty corridor.

Finally she heard something. Music. Long chords followed by short, repeating notes. Many instruments playing at the same time. Franni recognized the sound of violins and harpsichord. But there was a fast plucking by a lute that was at such a low pitch, it couldn't be a lute. The violins played the same note over and over, too. The strange music didn't make sense.

Apparently they weren't playing it right. The music stopped abruptly, and a gruff voice shouted, "Even! I want the semiquavers even! How many times must I tell you? You're no professional! Go back to your teacher like a little boy. Get out! Come back when you know how to play the theorbo."

Franni was glued to her spot in the hallway, afraid to move and wondering what a theorbo was. It didn't take long to find out. From a doorway a few feet in front of her, the end of a stringed instrument appeared. She recognized the many tuning pegs she'd seen on lutes. And then the neck, covered with more strings than she could count quickly, cut through by frets every inch or two. Franni kept staring, waiting to see who was carrying the lute. But the fretted neck and strings just kept on coming and coming. It was the longest neck she'd ever seen on any instrument, three times normal.

Finally a tall, slouchy man emerged from the doorway, his fist around the base of the instrument's gangly neck, and the body of the strange lute resting against his hip. Franni laughed at the silly sight. But as soon as she saw the wounded expression in the man's eyes, she clapped her hand over her mouth, ashamed. She tried to make it up to him by being friendly. Pointing at his six-foot-long lute, she whispered "Is that a theorbo?"

He nodded miserably, then scowled at his instrument as if it had betrayed him.

Franni pointed toward to doorway he'd just come out of. "Is that Maestro Monteverdi?"

The theorbo player seemed on the verge of tears when he nodded. He passed by Franni without a word and hurried down the hallway.

"Why is that girl here?" bellowed the same voice she'd heard yelling at the unfortunate musician. Peeking around the corner, Franni could see Giuseppe talking to a slim, bearded man in a black jacket and big white collar. Giuseppe turned and beckoned to someone. Franni took a few more steps in, and could see Alli straightening her dress and hair and moving forward with jerky steps. She looked completely terrified.

"Alessandra Ategnati is your name?" the slender man asked. Alli seemed frozen. "Are you the daughter of the great organ-maker, Costanzo Antegnati of Brescia?"

After a coughing fit, Alli managed to answer, "No, Maestro. I am his niece. I'm from Verona."

"Niece. Verona. Hmmm." The maestro seemed to be weighing the value of her ties to Constanzo. "Well, thanks to the smallpox, I can't be choosy. Can you read music? You won't have much time to learn your part. Performance in, what . . .?" He turned toward the director, Signore Striggio.

"Just under three weeks. The twenty-eighth day of May."

"Right. So, can you read music, girl?"

"Yes, Maestro."

"Are you a soprano?"

"Yes, Maestro." Alli accepted a booklet handed to her by a servant.

"Let's see if that's true. Sing the third song in that book."

"Oh, yes, sir!" Alli's hands shook as she turned the pages.

Franni's knees shook in sympathy. She wanted Alli to know she had a friend in the room. "Psst!" she whispered.

When Alli glanced over, Franni waved and smiled. The change in Alli was instantaneous. Her shoulders relaxed and her stride smoothed, although her eyes were still a bit wider than normal. Franni could understand. She wouldn't want to sing for that scary guy in the big collar.

Giuseppe helped Alli find a place to stand near the little band of instruments, then took his own seat and put his violin under his chin.

The Maestro raised his arms, and the musicians made ready to play. Alli shot one last hopeless look toward Franni at the back of the room, then focused her eyes on the trembling music pages. A long chord sounded, then some faster ones. The music had a nice, steady beat. Franni liked that much about it. Then Monteverdi pointed a long finger at Alli, who jumped when she saw it. "Now," he commanded.

She started in a tiny voice that sounded like somebody else. "Sing out!" bellowed the music director, stopping the band.

Alli yelped. Even safely at the back of the room, Franni jumped. She wished Alli would just run. Surely they could find another way to make a living in Mantua. But Alli was determined. She cleared her throat, squeaked, "Ready, Maestro," and cleared her throat again.

Monteverdi had raised his arms to start the music, when a man Franni hadn't even noticed suddenly stood up from one of the large armchairs scattered around the room. "Claudio," he said, "have a boy sing with her so we can see if she can carry a harmony."

The stunned look on Alli's face mirrored Franni's thoughts. Sing with a boy? A nice girl like Alli?

But Monteverdi nodded earnestly. "An excellent thought, Ottavio." He turned to the servant waiting in the corner. "Bring me a boy from the chorus." The servant sprinted from the room. While he was gone, Monteverdi ignored Alli, and took the opportunity to berate his violinists for their sloppy bowing. Franni could see Giuseppe sigh.

Within minutes, the servant returned, followed by a tall boy a bit older than Franni. He was rather handsome, with black hair and olive skin. At least, Franni thought he was rather handsome. Alli, on the other hand, seemed to think he was a god. Her hand moved to her heart. Her jaw fell open. And the boy, seeing her reaction, grinned the grin of a boy who knows girls think he looks like a god. Franni hated him immediately.

The man from the armchair approached the two singers. "This is a section from the opera *Orfeo,* which Maestro Monteverdi wrote last year. Remember, Luca and–Alli is your name, right?– in this chorus you represent spirits. Ghosts in the underworld. Now, carry on. Nice and clear, please."

"Yes, Signore Rinuccini," said the boy Luca with a bow.

"Yes, Signore Rinuccini," echoed Alli with a nervous smile.

After the man sat heavily in his armchair, they started the song together. Luca stood very close to Alli. Sure, he was sharing her sheet music, but Franni didn't think he needed to be *that* close. When Monteverdi pointed, they sang:

Man tries nothing in vain,
And Nature cannot protect herself from him.

"Spirits! You're supposed to be terrifying spirits in the Underworld," shouted Monteverdi, clapping his hands so loudly that one violinist dropped his bow in surprise. "You sound like love birds in the park!"

It was hard to hear this arrogant Maestro yell at Alli. And, what was worse, her sister was making goo-goo eyes at that boy singer. Franni decided she couldn't stand to watch the audition for another second.

CHAPTER 4

FRANNI'S PLAN WAS TO WAIT in the hallway until Alli came out of the audition. Tiptoeing from the room, she tried to figure out how many times her sister had been "in love." Back in Verona there had been a string of boys Alli doted on. Gianni, the violin-maker's apprentice, wiry with knobby knees and elbows. Stefanno, a palace guard. Werner, son of a German clockmaker, who had "Roman cheekbones," according to lovestruck Alli.

Each of these boys became Alli's obsession for six months or so. For each of them, she swore she would give her life or die of grief if he left her. Over each of them, she cried all night long (keeping Franni awake, of course). And one by one they began to bore her, and she abandoned each heartbroken youth with a brusque, thoughtless remark.

Alli never varied her pattern. And it always started with that sparkly-eyed gaze she'd given that brown-haired singer. Another obsession. Franni sighed as she closed the door behind her, thinking about what Alli would be like from now on, talking about nothing but this boy.

"Hey, there!" said a tall woman with deep creases in her forehead. She reached out and took Franni's arm. "They finally got us a new girl, eh? About time."

"What? No!" She struggled. She didn't want to be anybody's "new girl."

The woman released her. The creases on her face grew deeper, and Franni thought she might weep. "You're not the new girl? You don't know how to sew?"

That was quite an insult. Franni didn't enjoy sewing, but she was good at it. "Of course I can sew. My mother sewed dresses for the finest ladies in Verona. She taught me everything!"

The tears in the woman's eyes remained, but the face around them relaxed into a prayerful smile. "Oh, thank Heavens. So, you *are* the new girl!" She shook Franni's hand vigorously. "You're very young, but I started out young, as well. We seamstresses blossom early, eh?" She winked. Franni, not knowing what was happening, winked back. At least she wasn't frightened anymore. "Come with me, child." The woman took off down the hallway, with Franni running to keep up. Then she stopped again suddenly. "My name is Natalia Benotti. You will call me Signora Natalia. What's your name?"

Barely any sound came out when she answered, "Francesca."

"Francesca." Natalia said it flatly, like she was memorizing a street name.

"I mean Franni," Franni corrected. She always preferred her nickname.

"Fine. Franni, then. I'll call you anything you like, so long as you know how to sew gores in a petticoat."

As it happened, Franni did.

Natalia blabbered bitterly as she scurried down the hall. "Maestro M. wants it all gorgeous. Everything dripping with embroidery and lace. Jewels and ribbons sewn into the fabric. You'd think he was dressing the Greek gods themselves. Heavens, but such a huge project! When I was young and started in the theater, a shepherdess wore a simple frock." She changed her voice to a whisper. "Now that Vincenzo is the Duke, everyone on stage has to look like an emperor, even the servants." Natalia scrambled on ahead. "Oh, well. That's our job, I suppose. Let the patrons with the money and the artists with the visions tell us what they want, and we're supposed to find a way to make it real."

Franni had no idea what Signora Natalia was talking about, but she was interesting to listen to. By the time they turned off the hallway into a room, Franni had a smile on her face. This was much more fun than listening to her sister sing and swoon.

The room they entered was full of tables and piles of cloth. Costumes in various stages of completion hung on pegs and were draped over chairs. An elderly woman squinted over her needle.

"Donata," said Natalia, "meet Franni, the new girl."

The old woman stood and gave Franni a sweet, cheerful smile that warmed her to her toes. Her face was soft and round. "Welcome, dear. You need anything at all, you come right to old Donata. I've been sewing at the Palazzo since your parents were your age, I'll bet. There isn't a skein of thread I can't find."

"Thank you, ma'am," said Franni, curtsying.

"Just call me Donata, sweetheart." She smiled again.

"Donata, I need you to measure Signore Brandi again. He complained that his breeches in Act III don't fit right. You'll find him in the rehearsal hall."

"Going right away, Signora Natalia." Donata pushed herself up creakily and shuffled out the door.

Franni felt bad to see someone so old sent on errands, but Natalia was already thinking about something else. "Didn't I see that rascal Edgardo come in here earlier? Edgardo!" she called. "Edgardo? Are you here?"

Franni looked around. There was clearly nobody in the room, just a few tables and many piles of fabric. But Natalia tried again. "Hellooo? Edgardooo?"

"What is it?" snapped a nasal voice. "You know how busy I am fixing these wigs. This isn't even what I was hired for, I'll remind you."

Franni scanned the room again. She couldn't see anyone there.

"I've brought a new girl," Natalia said to a tower of bolts of blood-red silk. "She can sew the gores. Come out and meet her."

Franni got ready for anything. A ghost, a drunken man lying on the floor, maybe even a talking dog. But she was not prepared for Edgardo. Out from behind the red fabric came a miniature man. He was quite a bit shorter than Franni, but had whiskers on his chin, proving he was no child. "Ha!" she cried, before she could stop herself. She clapped her hand over her mouth.

The little man's legs were so short that he waddled. And he waddled right up to Franni. "Ha, yourself. You're no prize. Look at how frizzy your hair is!"

Franni's hands went automatically to her scalp and pushed her unruly hair back into her headband. "I can't help it," she whined.

"Well, I can't help being shorter than a pony's behind." Franni gasped, surprised by the crude reference. The dwarf tried to fold his arms, but they weren't quite long enough to cross his chest. "Here's the deal: I won't make fun of your hair if you don't make fun of my height." There was a glint of challenge in his eye.

Franni liked this adorable, grouchy fellow immensely. She wanted to put her arms around him. But she could tell he'd hate that. She would have hated it, too, if the roles had been reversed. "Deal," she said. "I'm Franni."

He gave a courtly bow, a very practiced bow. Franni was impressed. "Pleased to make your acquaintance, Franni. I'm Edgardo. I was hired for my expertise at theatrical sets, but, as you can see," he spun a gray wig around his index finger, "I'm valued for my other skills as well. In general, I try to get underfoot as much as possible." He stopped, his eyebrows raised in expectation. Franni held her breath and bit her cheeks. "You may laugh when *I* make a joke about being short."

She let out the laugh she'd been holding in, and Edgardo grinned and nodded. His sense of humor made Franni think of her father in the happiest way possible.

Natalia had been buzzing around the room, moving bolts of cloth, pulling supplies from boxes, and clearing off a table. "Here, Franni. This will be your work space."

It was a far cry from the large oak table she'd shared in her mother's studio, but Franni thought she'd better not complain. "What will I be sewing?" She reached out for the nearest cloth, a jewel-like blue (the color her mother once called "azure") that shimmered in the afternoon light pouring through the windows. But Natalia swatted her hand away.

"Not that. I think we'd better test you out before we let you sew the Arabian silk. Here." She handed Franni a few feet of simple white linen cloth. "Make an apron."

That was a real challenge for Franni. She'd never sewn anything completely by herself before, but she knew she could do it. She tried to imagine an apron. "There's not much cloth."

"That's part of the test," said Natalia. "We never have enough materials to work with, so we have to get clever about using them."

"Okay," said Franni, frowning with concentration. "How big should the apron be?"

Edgardo did a fancy twirl, landing in front of her with his index finger pressed to his chin. He batted his eyelashes. "How about making it for me? That shouldn't take too much fabric."

While Franni giggled, Natalia rolled her eyes. "I have work to do. Make the apron for this miniature fool. All the same to me, so long as it fits him well. I'll be back in a while to check on your progress, Franni. If you do a decent job, I'll hire you for a florin a week."

Franni's heart soared at the thought of making money. She and Alli wouldn't have to beg anymore! "Oh,thank you, *thank* you, Signora Natalia," said Franni, curtsying.

But Natalia just harumphed and headed toward the door. "You won't thank me for long, child," she said, and went out, closing the door behind her.

Franni's face must have fallen like her spirits, because Edgardo reached out a stubby arm and patted her hand. "Never mind the old grouse," he said. "You and I, we'll have a fine time together. Now, let's get to work on that apron, so you can become an official employee of the Duke of Mantua."

"Become a what?"

Edgardo laughed. "Who do you think will be paying your enormous salary? It will come from the Duke's coffers." Leaning toward her, he added, "Not that there's much gold left in those coffers. Vincenzo spends like a drunken sailor lost in a brothel."

Franni burst out laughing, surprised all over again by this little man's coarse humor. She'd never heard such naughty things coming from such an educated mouth. His elegant pronunciation made him sound like a scholar. He bowed like a courtier. But he behaved like a back-street urchin. She'd never met anyone like him.

Edgardo held up his arms, dangling a measuring tape. "Come on, then. Measure me." When Franni stepped closer, she towered over him. It was like pretending to sew clothes for a large doll. Again Franni fought the urge to hug Edgardo. Instead, she measured the distance from his collarbone to his knee.

Next, she needed to know the distance around his waist. "Raise your arms higher, please," she said, trying to sound as professional as possible.

When he did so, the left side of his shirt came untucked. "Oh, dear. I'm all askew. Can't have that!" he muttered, blushing. He shoved the shirttail quickly back into his trousers.

Understanding that he must be very shy around girls, Franni turned away to let him put himself together and settle down. Her mother had sometimes been in situations like this, when Franni was little and would sit in the sewing room and watch her work. So now Franni tried the light conversational style her mother used to use to put her clients at ease.

"Have you always lived in Mantua?" she asked, busying herself laying out the cloth and finding a pair of scissors.

"Why do you want to know that?" Edgardo practically shrieked.

This was not going at all as planned. Franni fought back tears. "I'm so sorry," she said. "I didn't mean to make you feel uncomfortable." She wiped her face with the back of her hands. "You shouldn't be so shy. I think you're very nice." She thought hard for something positive to say. "And you have a noble nose."

Edgardo froze. They stared at each other. Franni couldn't believe things had gone so wrong, so quickly, and she didn't dare make the next move. It was sure to be a disaster, whatever she tried. Finally Edgardo's mouth softened into a grin. "I think you're nice, too, Franni. And I think your nose looks like a snail. I'm going to call you Snailnose."

A nickname! It wouldn't have been the one she preferred, but Franni was so glad to have Edgardo joking with her that she didn't mind. She tried to keep things friendly. "My sister and I just arrived from Verona," she offered.

"Nice town, Verona," said Edgardo. "I've lived all over the place, but I grew up in Monza."

Franni smiled, relieved he was speaking to her. "Where's that?"

"Near Milan, in Lombardy."

She nodded. "My uncle lives in Lombardy, too. In Brescia."

"That's nice." The conversation tapered off into an awkward silence. Edgardo turned his attention to the pile of wigs he was mending. Franni laid out the material to start the apron she was supposed to make. She was dying to ask how Edgardo learned how to make wigs, but she didn't want to offend him.

She couldn't think of anything to say or ask that wouldn't sound like she was prying. So, instead, she invented his story. Franni imagined that Edgardo was the son of a tailor in the little town of Monza. She pictured it as a tiny, quaint town. He was very skilled at sewing clothes, but his father wouldn't let him work in his shop because he was so short that he made the wealthy customers uncomfortable. So, when he was sixteen, he ran away to Mantua. The Duke, who loved the theater, hired him to sew costumes. That way only the musicians and other servants would see him.

"What are you grinning at?" Edgardo asked. Franni was so surprised to hear him speak that she pricked her finger.

"Nothing!"

"Hmmm. You're a secretive girl. I like that." He gave a little bow. "It's been a great pleasure meeting you, Franni. I need to go check on the sets I've designed. The crew, if I may say, are a bunch of oafs and idiots, so I have to watch them at every turn. Your apron is looking very stylish, and I'm sure Natalia will hire you. Good afternoon."

Franni didn't know what to make of the odd little man. She wondered if he'd really been there at all. Alone in the costume workshop, she could hear strains of music, and occasionally voices, wafting through the halls. She lost herself in the sewing and in her imagination. Natalia came in once, nodded approvingly, and lit some candles for her.

Hours passed. Franni was getting very hungry, and was about to go in search of that room filled with food. Just as she stood up, she heard Alli's voice out in the hallway. Her sister sounded distressed, so Franni ran from the room.

"I can't believe it!" Alli wailed, her hand to her forehead.

That boy who had been singing with her walked in a nervous circle. That's what most people did when Alli got upset. He sputtered out half a sentence. "I'm sure Maestro Monteverdi thought . . ."

Alli turned on him. "Luca! How dare you tell me what he thought! It's obvious what he thought."

"Alli, what is it?" Franni asked fearfully. She assumed the composer had decided he couldn't use Alli. She wanted to assure Alli that they would be making some money from her sewing, but she didn't. Franni knew better than to turn the conversation to herself when her sister was feeling hurt. To Luca she said, "I'm Franni, Alli's sister."

"I'm Luca de Rore," said the young man. "Maestro liked your sister's voice."

"But he put me in the *chorus*." Alli spat out that word like venom. "He should have given me the *lead*."

CHAPTER 5

NATALIA'S SPINSTER SISTER, MARIA, ran a boarding house for women who worked in the theater. Because the Duke of Mantua encouraged theater in his city, there were plenty of women staying there already. Still, Maria found a small room for Franni and Alli to share. The house wasn't far from the Palazzo, so getting to work would be an easy walk.

Completely exhausted after their first day of work, the sisters slept soundly Friday night.

"Show me your letter," Maria said to Franni the next day. "Natalia vouched for you, but I need proof of your employment so I know you can pay your rent."

"What letter, Signora?" asked Franni.

Alli stepped forward. "I've got them." She pulled two pieces of fine linen paper from her purse. They glittered when she unfolded them.

"Are those ours? Let me see!" said Franni. She snatched them away. One of them claimed that Alessandra Antegnati was a "Participant in the Chorus for a Theatrical Entertainment by Maestro Monteverdi." Alli snatched that one back.

Franni examined the other letter, then read aloud. "This establishes Francesca Antegnati as an Assistant Seamstress of Clothing for the Theatrical Works under the Auspices of his Most Serene Highness, Vincenzo Gonzaga, Duke of Mantua."

Franni arched her eyebrows, trying to look important. "Did you see this stationery?" She ran her fingers over the ornate ducal signia. "Is that real gold?"

"It's lovely, dear," laughed Maria, "and I'm sure it is real gold. Duke Gonzaga probably gilds his bread in real gold."

Several women in the room laughed and nodded to each other.

Maria said, "Wait in the parlor, and I'll bring some food."

That sounded good to Franni. She continued to admire the seal as she followed Alli along a hallway. "Real gold. How much do you think this one piece of paper is worth? Look at the beautiful penmanship. I didn't know it was possible to write so perfectly." Jogging a few paces, she caught up with Alli as they entered the parlor. A young woman in a startling red dress was seated in the corner.

Alli gasped. Franni kept on chattering. "I mean, you remember Papa's handwriting? Ha! So messy. Do you think the Duke has a person who does nothing but write pretty letters for him all day long?"

Alli turned and snapped at Franni. "I don't know! How would I know?"

At first, Franni was hurt, but she saw Alli stealing glances at her own letter, her eyes lighting up. As usual, Alli was putting on a show of not caring when she actually cared quite a lot. Alli made a little curtsy to the red-dressed woman. "You'll have to excuse my sister. She's very excitable. I guess it's the thrill of being in Mantua."

She says I'm *excitable*, thought Franni. *Look who's talking.* But she knew better than to say anything. She didn't like the woman in the red dress. Her face was squashed, as if she were always feeling pressed in by life.

"I'm Iulia," said the woman. She didn't rise, which Franni thought was very rude.

"Hi, I'm, um, I'm Alli, um, and this is my little sister, Franni, and it's so nice to meet you, and I just *know* we're going to be friends!"

Her sister was blathering like an idiot. If Franni could have sunk down into the floor, she would have done so gladly.

But Alli wasn't finished. "I'm singing with Maestro Monteverdi. He has a new theatrical entertainment with music. It's called–"

"*Arianna.*" Iulia yawned as she said it. "I've been in the chorus on that show since January."

"January?" Alli's shoulders slumped. "That's four whole months!"

Franni was relieved Alli no longer had anything to brag about. Now she could get a word in. "Shouldn't you have performed it by now?"

Iulia laughed. "Oh, please. It's been one problem after another." She motioned for Alli to sit down on the sofa, but ignored Franni. "We were supposed to perform it in early March, during the Carnival festival before Lent. But then the whole wedding got postponed until late May."

This struck Franni as very odd. "Weren't they sure they loved each other?"

Iulia laughed again. She had a harsh laugh that did not make Franni want to laugh with her. "With dukes and princesses, love has nothing to do with it."

Alli put her hand to her heart. "That's not really true, is it? If a duke loved me, I would love him back."

"What a nice fantasy." Iulia patted Alli on the knee like a big sister.

Franni felt a pang of jealousy, but was distracted by the determination on Alli's face. "I'll get my duke," said Alli. "You'll see."

Not wanting to hear another speech about what perfect husbands dukes made, Franni steered the conversation back to *Arianna*. "So, why *did* they move the wedding to May?"

Standing up, Iulia curtsied deeply, as if to an invisible nobleman. "His Most Serene Highness decided there was already too much going in March." She straightened up and put her hand on her hip. "His Highness also thought that the people of Mantua would be bored in May, and need entertainment."

"Well," said Alli, "I guess his Highness truly cares about his people."

"Don't you believe it." A voice behind Franni surprised her. It was Maria, entering the room with a tray of snacks.

Maria shook her head. "Pardon my frankness, but that Duke just didn't want Mantua to be distracted from his giant party."

Alli clasped her hands together. "Will it really be such a giant party?"

Another woman, tall with braided black hair, entered the room. "Giant party is right. It's supposed to last for a week. There will be several theatrical performances, all commissioned just for the celebration." She gave Franni a pleasant smile. "I'm Linda. Welcome, girls."

"Thanks!" Franni was happy to see someone with a friendlier face than Iulia's. "Are you a singer, too?"

"Actress," said Linda. "Sing a little when I have to." She poured herself a glass of wine and sat down. "I've been in the Mantua theater since I was your age. And I've worked for three different Gonzaga dukes. I can tell you," she added with a wink, "Vincenzo wants to be the most spectacular, glamorous duke the world has ever seen."

"No matter how much it costs the city of Mantua." Maria sighed and shook her head.

Franni thought about the real gold on her letter.

Leaning in close to Iulia, Alli said, "Who do you think the maestro will hire to play Arianna, now that the Lord has taken poor Madame, er—"

"Madame Catarina Martinelli. Yes, she died of the smallpox, poor thing." Iulia spoke in a serious tone. "May she rest in peace." Everyone crossed herself. Franni mumbled a quick prayer for the singer who'd died. Iulia's face widened into an impish grinned. "Well, it's not going to be you or me."

"Probably someone from Florence," said Linda, veteran of the theater. "Maestro Monteverdi loves those Florentine singers."

The girls continued to chat. Franni felt left out. She didn't belong in this conversation. Or in this house. Or in the town of Mantua. The more she thought about how out of place she was, the sadder Franni became. She missed Verona. She missed her friends. She missed her house. But, most of all, she missed her mother.

Franni ran up the stairs to their room and unbuckled her satchel. There wasn't much in it. They'd had very little time to pack, and they couldn't have carried much on foot, anyway.

Wiping the hot tears from her eyes, Franni reached in and felt around until her fingers touched something soft and familiar. It was a small doll her mother had made of scraps of fabric. The doll was oddly shaped, looking like a combination of a baby, a bear, and a cat. It was made from many mismatched patterns of cloth. Although it was kind of ugly, Franni had kept it since she was five. Now it was her only physical remembrance of her mother. That doll had soaked up a lot of Franni's tears, but it always seem ready to help her get through another tough day.

"Babbo," she said gently to the doll, "I'm not sure I like it here." Closing her eyes, Franni pressed Babbo to her forehead. "Oh, Mama and Papa, don't let Alli go astray. I don't like the people she's making friends with. But I'm just her little sister. She doesn't care what I think. Please guide her from Heaven."

The sound of women singing drifted up the stairs. Franni realized Alli and Iulia must be practicing their music for Maestro Monteverdi. But one phrase from the melody reminded Franni of a song their father used to sing. Franni sang it now to Babbo. Her voice shook, and she knew she was out of tune, but it didn't matter.

Up in the skies you see the sun
Beginning a day all bright and new.
Open your eyes, my precious one,
And learn what the day will bring to you.

She sang it again. How many times had she heard her father sing it? A hundred? He'd used it to put her to sleep when she was a baby and comfort her when she got a little older. But now, when she sang it to herself, the words had a new meaning.

Franni knew what she had to do. Just like it said in the song, she had to open up her eyes and really look at Mantua. There might be all sorts of wonderful friends and adventures waiting for her, but she'd never find them if she didn't look.

It was Saturday, and Natalia had said Franni didn't need to return to work until Monday. "Maybe I should go outside and explore," she said to Babbo. "Maybe Alli and I need a day off from each other. She's made some new friends, and now it's my turn." Franni kissed Babbo on the head and tucked him deep inside her satchel. "I'll be back soon."

Franni walked down the stairs and paused at the parlor doorway. She waited for the right moment to interrupt the conversation and tell Alli she was going out.

"Excuse me, honey." A woman Franni didn't know wanted to get past her. Franni watched her enter the room with a comical flourish. Everyone hurried up to greet her and introduce Alli. They all ignored Franni. In no time, the women had gone back to laughing and gossiping over tea, wine, and cakes.

Alli appeared to be having a delightful afternoon. She wasn't looking around for her only sister. She didn't seem to be wondering how Franni was faring in the strange new place. *I guess she won't miss me,* thought Franni, feeling tears form in her eyes again. As she walked toward the front door, she could still hear Alli's delicate laughter and Iulia's brash guffaws ringing through the house.

The bright sunshine on the paving stones cheered Franni the moment she got outside. She considered heading off down one of the many narrow streets. Peering down one of them, she could see a bakery, with a little dog begging at its entrance. But she had no money (they'd been promised their first wages the following week), and she knew there was no point in getting lost.

She decided it made sense to follow the route to the Palazzo, but to try it on her own. Franni figured the same streets would look completely different if she weren't following in her sister's shadow.

She was right. She noticed dogs, horses, an inn, a shoemaker's. She stopped into a toymaker's shop, but the proprietor chased her out.

"Shoo, *ragazza*! Urchin!"

"Urchin!" she repeated, backing out of the store. It was quite an eye-opener to be called that. She'd seen her father chase orphan boys out of his warehouse back in Verona. "Ragazzi!" he would shout, shaking a broom at them. Franni used to think it was funny. It had never occurred to her that those little boys were people just like her.

She was lost in these thoughts when she noticed the crowd swirling around her.

"Who are they?" a woman asked.

"They're soldiers, riding in from the north," said a short man in a wide leather hat.

"They're going to read a message in front of the Palazzo," a teenaged boy called up to a girl in a window. "I heard they were wearing the colors of Bergamo."

"Bergamo! It's not war they're announcing, is it?" an old woman asked, hugging herself. "Oh, gracious, it can't be a war!"

Some little children held hands and danced in a chain, singing, "Bergamo, Bergamo, Bergamo!"

Franni let herself be swept along to the Palazzo. Whatever was going on, she didn't want to miss it. There was a festive atmosphere, even though nobody quite knew what was happening. As they neared the Palazzo, the crowed got so thick that Franni couldn't see a thing. All around her people's arms and backs closed in around her. Then she noticed the perfect place to climb up for a better view. She got a good foothold on a curly marble banister and hoisted herself up a good foot above everyone's heads.

She could see the team of riders now, eight of them on huge stallions. The six men in the center and their horses were draped in purple and red silks. The riders on either end wore yellow and green, which Franni recognized as the colors of Mantua.

One of the purple and red riders tooted on a small trumpet. The crowd's roar quieted to a hum.

"Hear ye, citizens of Mantua!" he cried from his saddle. "I bear news of a most urgent nature."

CHAPTER 6

THE CROWD FELL SILENT. People held their breath and clasped their hands together with anticipation. This certainly was more exciting than listening to theater gossip back at Maria's house! Franni folded her arms, ready for anything the messenger might say.

The messenger unfurled a large piece of paper. "We seek the heir to the Dukedom of Bergamo," he shouted.

"What's that got to do with us?" some wag called out. "This is Mantua. Shouldn't you be looking for your duke in Bergamo?"

A few people laughed, but more shushed him. The messenger, glaring at the rude fellow, cleared his throat and continued reading out his announcement. "The rightful heir is missing. If he does not claim his title by Wednesday, the twenty-eighth day of May, his rights will be forfeit and the House of Gritti will take control of the ducal palace." He looked up. "Believe me, that Gritti family will take power by force, if necessary. They're a determined bunch."

"Keep your troubles up in Bergamo where they belong," somebody near Franni called out. "We've got enough troubles of our own."

The messenger grimaced and continued. "The heir has not lived in Bergamo since he was an infant. He is the child of Lady Alma D'Espelina, daughter of the late beloved Duke Alfonzo D'Espelina."

"I'll bet you don't know who the father is," taunted the wag.

The messenger glared daggers at the crowd. "Her husband, of course! Sadly, he died in the Turkish wars before the baby was born. The mother died in childbirth."

Franni wanted to learn more about this missing duke. "What does he look like?" she called to the messenger.

Someone else agreed, "Yes, tell us what he looks like."

The messenger held the document to eye level and read. "The rightful heir was given to a monastery as an infant, so his exact appearance is unknown."

A murmur started to grow from the crowd, but the messenger cut through it. "*However,* his father was tall and broad-shouldered, with wavy brown hair. And we know he has a birthmark shaped like a fish on the right side of his lower back."

"Maybe he swam away," joked a man in a leather blacksmith's apron. "We do have a lot of lakes in Mantua, so I can see why you're here."

The crowd laughed, but Franni could tell they were intrigued. People turned to those near them to discuss the situation, and she could hear the word "birthmark" pop up here and there.

"Shouldn't you ask at the monastery?" somebody asked.

"Of course, we started there," said the messenger, sounding sick of the whole business. "They say he ran away as a child."

"And why do you think he's in Mantua?" asked another man.

"Besides the lakes?" added the woman next to him.

Now the messenger ran his fingers through his hair. "Ahem. Well, to be honest, we've tried every town between here and Bergamo. Every town in the Venetian province, in fact. You might say we're expanding our search."

"Ha!" The wag raised his hands in triumph. "You have no idea whether he's here." A lot of people snickered. "I knew it!"

"At least it makes for a bit of entertainment," reasoned an elderly man in a purple hat.

"What's this duke fella's name?" a woman asked.

"His true name," read the messenger, "is Marco Coriglio D'Espelina, the Second." He looked up. "But we don't know what he's been calling himself, of course." More laughter.

Franni called out another question. "Where should we look for him?"

The answer to this was apparently also on the paper, which surprised her. The messenger read, "The rightful Duke will most likely try to blend in with the lower classes. But he is of noble birth and raised by monks, so he is likely to be above average in skill and intelligence."

Once the crowd stopped laughing at that, they got caught up in the idea of a duke hiding in their midst. Franni heard people claiming they had a neighbor or cousin or physician or tailor with broad shoulders and wavy brown hair. There were even a few men in the crowd who fit that description. "Can you prove you were born in Mantua?" one woman asked her husband. It was a very confusing scene, and Franni wanted to narrow down the choices.

"How old is he?" she yelled out, hoping to be heard above the chaos.

The people around her shushed each other and waited for the messenger to read his answer. "Duke Marco Coriglio D'Espelina, the Second, was born on the twenty-fourth day of January, in the year of our Lord fifteen-hundred and eighty seven."

Franni tried to figure out what that meant, but she'd never been very good at subtraction. Fortunately, a young man toward the back of the crowd said, "So, he's twenty-one."

"As you say, sir." The messenger raised his eyebrows, as if he hadn't figured that out before.

A broad-hipped woman pushed her way to the front. Wagging a finger upward at the mounted messenger, she said, "I have the most important question of all."

Everyone fell silent, straining to hear.

"Why should we help you find this duke. What's it to us? Eh?"

Hundreds of people murmured their agreement at the importance of this question, and there were a few catcalls, too. But the messenger was prepared. Sitting up even straighter in the saddle, he held up one hand to quiet the masses.

"The town of Bergamo appeals to your decency. If this Marco is not found and brought home by the twenty-eighth of May, there will surely be bloodshed as the D'Espelina family tries to defend its rule from the rival family."

The woman shook her fist. "Mantua doesn't want any part of your battles." A cry arose from the crowd. Franni watched, amazed by how angry everyone seemed. People were beginning to step forward, closing in on the poor messenger. He raised his hands with this palms outward, begging for patience.

"Hear ye! Great City of Mantua! Anyone who helps our search party successfully identify the Duke will be awarded from the coffers of the Bergamo trust, guaranteed by the State of Venice, a sum of two thousand five hundred ducats . . ."

The messenger continued reading, but his words were drowned out by the whooping and hollering of the crowd.

Franni couldn't help laughing at the change in the citizens once they knew they could get money for finding the duke. Then she had another amusing though. *Wait until Alli finds out about this. Maybe she can get herself a duke and the reward money at the same time.*

It was a nice idea, actually. Alli would be happy, Franni wouldn't have to sew costumes, and they could both leave Mantua. Franni decided to do her best to find the duke, just so Alli could marry him.

It seemed like a great plan, and she could tell from the chatter around her that everyone in town was planning the same thing. But Franni was sure that, if they put their heads together, she and Alli could find the duke faster than any of these silly Mantuan people. Her anger toward her sister forgotten, she bounded through the narrow streets. She pushed her way past wide-gesturing gossips and keen-eyed boys scoping out everyone who walked by.

"There's no way I can be the duke," she said to one ambitious youth who peered at her too closely. "I'm a girl, in case you hadn't noticed." He seemed disappointed when he stepped back to let her pass.

Franni couldn't wait to get back to the house and tell Alli about the duke-in-hiding. She imagined how she and her sister would laugh and scheme. As she walked, Franni's memory turned back to happier times.

One Christmas in Verona, she and Alli had sneaked away from their parents after Mass. They'd giggled, sliding along the slushy streets, counting how many parish churches were ringing their bells. (They'd given up at twenty.) From a street vendor, Alli had bought them fried buns drizzled with honey, which steamed in the frigid air. What a glorious day that had been.

The wonderful memory gave Franni new energy, and she was running by the time Maria's house was in view. She flew through the front door. "Alli! Alli!" Peeking into the parlor, she saw her sister there. "Oh, Alli, you'll never guess what this messenger announced by the Palazzo. He was from the town of Bergamo, up north, and he said—"

Franni stopped cold, stunned by the strained look on Alli's face. "What happened?" she asked, terrified of the news she might hear.

Alli stood, her fists clenched. "What do you mean, 'What happened?'" The two other women in the parlor exchanged a glance and slipped out of the room. "Where have you *been*, Francesca?"

The sound of her full name sent a shot of pain through Franni's heart. Alli suddenly turned into a cruel version of their mother, like she was under some twisted enchantment. "I couldn't find you anywhere," Alli said, her eyes hard and wild. "I thought you'd been kidnapped. How *dare* you leave his house without telling me?"

All Franni's feelings of loneliness and neglect came flying back. "What do you care where I was? All you care about is *you.*" She pointed an accusing finger at Alli. "Your stupid boys and your stupid singing."

"My singing is paying the rent, isn't it?"

"It's fine for you, getting to sing and wear all those pretty costumes. I have to sit in a dark room sewing those dresses and talking to dwarves." Immediately Franni regretted saying such a thing. She liked Edgardo, and his height didn't bother her. She was just in such an awful mood that there was nothing in the world she didn't despise at the moment. She blamed Alli for her own cruel words. "You drive me crazy. You make me say things I don't mean. Why do I have to be stuck with you? You're not my mama! Why did Mama and Papa both have to die? It's not fair!"

Franni grabbed a pile of sheet music and held it above her head with both hands gripping one side. She made a little tearing motion as a threat. "I'll do it. I swear I'll do it if you make me stay here."

Like a cornered cat, Alli swung her hands out and practically hissed. "Go ahead, you spoiled brat. What do I care? I don't need that lame chorus music. I'll get the lead role, anyway. Just you wait and see."

Barely knowing what she was doing, Franni dropped the music, ran out of the parlor and bounded up the stairs. Everything around her looked blurry, and her head throbbed and burned like it was caught in a fireplace. Her anger swallowed her up, and all she wanted was somebody to blame. She lurched into their room and grabbed Alli's travel satchel from the floor. Plunging her hand in, she pulled out Alli's blue dress, her only spare clothing. Franni took two fistfuls of the material and yanked her hands in opposite directions.

Pop-pop-pop went a hundred stitches. The dress now had a huge hole in the bodice. Franni sat on the edge of the bed and looked at the ripped garment in her shaking hands. She couldn't believe she'd just done such a thing. "Oh, Alli—," she began, but she couldn't say another word. She just sobbed and sobbed. Soon she realized that Alli's arms were around her, and her sister was sobbing, too.

It felt good to cry, and after a while they both calmed down. "I can fix this," Franni said, examining the dress. "It's just along the seam."

"Okay," Alli said quietly.

"Come on, Alli," Franni pleaded. "Let's go to Brescia. There's lots of music there. You can sing for Uncle Costanzo. I bet he'll give you a job in the church where he works."

Alli just folded her arms, so Franni tried a different approach. "Or we can go to the town of Monza and be farmers."

"Farmers!" exclaimed Alli, clearly trying not to smile.

Wiping her eyes and sniffling, Franni looked at the floor. "Somebody told me Monza is nice."

Alli sighed. "We can't just keep moving around. You understand that, right? At least here we have work."

"You get to sing, but I have to sew."

"Franni-Anni-Anni," the older girl cooed, using a nickname Franni hadn't heard since she was four or five, "let's take this one step at a time. Let's just agree to stay here until the performance of *Arianna* at the end of May."

"Three weeks? I have to sew for three whole weeks?"

"It's less than three weeks. And you're really good at it. You have a gift."

"That doesn't mean I like it. Why do we have to stay here? It's because of that boy, Luca, isn't it?"

"Never mind Luca. Luca doesn't matter."

Franni wasn't buying it. "You like him. You think he's cute." She saw Alli flutter her eyelids, a dead giveaway.

"He really thinks he can get me a better part in *Arianna,*" Alli said. Reaching out, she took Franni's hands. "I guess he has connections. Who knows? Maybe if I get a bigger role, the Duke will notice me, and we'll get rich."

"The Duke!" Franni smacked her forehead. "I completely forgot to tell you about the Duke."

Clasping her hands to her heart, Alli leaned forward. "What about Duke Gonzaga? He's not ill, is he?"

"No, not the Duke of Mantua. The Duke of Bergamo."

Alli wrinkled her nose. "Bergamo?"

"A messenger came to town while I was out. He said the heir to the dukedom is missing, and they think he might be hiding out in Mantua."

"Oh, how thrilling!" Alli cried. "A missing duke!"

"The messenger says he was taken to a monastery as a baby. They don't even know who his father was, but his mother was in the Duke's family."

"So, he has ducal blood through his mother?" Alli was breathing hard, as if this were the most fascinating story she'd ever heard.

"I guess so. But he ran away from the monastery. That's where they lose the trail."

"Oh, the poor thing. They must have mistreated him."

Shaking her head, Franni said, "Honestly, I think you're already in love with him. All anyone has to say is 'Duke,' and you're a goner."

There was no trace of joking on Alli's face. "Franni, we have to find him."

And I haven't even mentioned the reward yet, Franni thought with a smile. "I don't supposed you've noticed any tall, mysterious twenty-one-year-old guys with wavy brown hair."

Rather than laughing, Alli looked earnestly into the distance. Then her eyes grew as big as windows, and she clapped her palms against her cheeks. "Luca!"

CHAPTER 7

INTO THE WEE HOURS OF the morning Franni and Alli whispered about Luca.

"It has to be him," Alli argued. "I mean, look at him! Has anyone ever looked so noble?"

But Franni just wasn't convinced. "What are the chances? They've been looking for him in every town. It's impossible that we would happen to know him."

"It's not impossible," Alli objected. The moonlight shining through the bedroom window made her eyes sparkle. "Think about it, Franni. He's a person out in the world. He has to be somewhere. And he must talk to people and get to know them in his everyday life. Somebody knows this duke. And it just happens to be us. I don't see anything impossible about it."

Franni looked at her sister's moonlit face. She saw her father's features there, just for a second. "Maybe it's not impossible. I suppose we could watch him at work next week and see what we think." She shrugged. "Or maybe he'll be gone."

Alli bolted up in bed. "Gone?"

"If he's the Duke, and he knows everyone's looking at him, wouldn't he leave town?" Franni pictured herself riding on the back of his horse. Not so she could run away and marry him like Alli wanted, but just so she could go have an adventure somewhere else.

"He won't leave, he won't leave." Alli kept repeating this as she lay back onto her pillow. "He won't leave, he won't leave."

"Goodnight, Alli."

Sunday seemed to drag on forever. Much as she hated to admit it, Franni was caught up in this missing Duke business. And it was all anyone could talk about. The girls attended church with the other residents of Maria's house. Everyone was chattering low, even during the service. Franni kept hearing the word "duke," usually followed by the word "reward." Whoever this man was, he wouldn't be missing for long with all these greedy eyes searching for him.

On Monday morning they left early for rehearsals at the Palazzo. Everyone they passed on the streets was whispering. Franni felt like she was being scrutinized by every pair of eyes. On the other hand, she found herself peering closely at everyone else. Could *that* be the duke? Did *that* person know where the duke was?

"Of course the duke could have dyed his hair blond," an old man was saying as they neared the Palazzo. Franni recognized him from the scenery crew.

"How do you do that?" asked a very blond woman.

She looks like she already knows, thought Franni. But she said nothing.

"You grind up walnut shells and bark from the walnut tree." The man held the door for the blond woman, Franni, and Alli. "Cook them down in some water, then mix in alum crystals and oak apples."

"What are oak apples?" asked Alli.

"A kind of nest for insect eggs you find on trees. So you mix that in, too, and let it steep for a few days."

"How fascinating!" said the blond woman, patting her own hair gingerly with her fingertips.

"Then you just put it on your head?" Franni asked.

The man smiled at her. "You smear it on the hair and leave it in for two days. The hardest part comes next. You have to comb out all the crusty bits that are stuck on the strands."

The blond woman addressed Alli. “If you want a more golden color, you should add a little henna mixed with crocus root and dragon’s blood.”

“Dragon’s blood?” exclaimed Iulia, who seemed to come out of nowhere.

Franni laughed. “Don’t worry, it’s not from dragons. It’s just bright red dye. They make it out of reeds.”

The man gave her a funny look. “How do you know that, child?”

Franni didn’t feel like saying the truth, which was that her mother was a dressmaker and knew all about dyeing cloth. That might have led the old man to ask about her mother, and Franni didn’t feel like telling everyone Mama was dead.

Fortunately, Alli seemed to sense the problem. She put one arm around Franni to pull her away, and said to the man and the blond woman, “That’s my sister, all right. She soaks up all kinds of odd information. Drives us all crazy with it.”

Franni let herself be herded into the room where there was always food on offer. “Thanks,” she mumbled to Alli, without looking at her.

Alli handed her a sweetroll. “I miss her, too,” she whispered.

She really is a good sister, Franni thought gratefully.

Somehow Iulia was there with them again. She seemed to be everywhere. “Psst!” she said in a clownish whisper that would have worked well in a comedy on the stage. “I have a secret. Where can we talk?”

“In the sewing room,” Alli volunteered, without asking Franni if it was okay. Then again, maybe Alli wasn’t such a good sister. “I have a secret, too.”

“Ooh, can I come?” A woman a little older than Alli stood next to the table of sweet rolls and rubbed her hands together. “I love secrets.”

“This is Georgia,” said Iulia. “Meet Alli. She sings in the chorus, too. Georgia should be in on the secret.” Nobody bothered to introduce Franni. All she could do was tag along as the clique of choristers bustled down the hallway to the sewing room.

When they arrived, Natalia was busy chewing out the old seamstress Donata about an uneven hemline. When she saw Franni and the singers, Franni flinched, readying herself for anything. But Natalia's face relaxed.

"Oh, very clever to bring the girls here for their fittings at the start of the day. We always get so over-run with measuring in the afternoons." Natalia reached for a leather-bound notebook on the table and handed it to a very puzzled Franni. "Just jot the numbers in here, dear." And she left the room.

Donata, her wrinkled eyes red with tears, excused herself and went into an adjoining chamber. Alli and her friends started up their frenetic gossiping the moment the door closed.

"It's about the Duke, right?" Georgia started. "What do you think?"

"I bet I know who it is," Iulia said proudly.

"No, I bet *I* do," said Alli. "But you go first."

Franni, trying not to groan, rummaged among the piles of material for a measuring tape.

"Both of you say your ideas at the same time," suggested Georgia. "One, two, three . . . *go*!"

"Luca!" Iulia and Alli said at once.

"Goodness!" Franni couldn't help being impressed. She'd thought her sister's crush on the young tenor had clouded her judgment. But Iulia seemed just as sure. "Why do you think that?" Franni asked.

"*Franni*," Alli warned, "This is a grown-up discussion."

But Iulia seemed pleased about the question. She lifted her arms high in the air as she answered, so Franni could measure her waist. "I saw his birthmark," she whispered. "On his lower back. It's shaped like a fish."

Everyone gasped, including Franni.

"How did you manage to see . . .?" Georgia stammered. "Oh, you must tell us every little thing!"

"You didn't do anything you'll regret, did you?" Alli asked with a concern that Franni thought did her credit.

Iulia giggled demurely. "Don't be so silly, silly-puss. It was on Sunday . . ."

"The Lord's day?" Georgia excaimed. "How *could* you?"

"Seriously, I didn't do anything wrong." Iulia seemed flustered. "I was visiting Mirella d'Alba after Mass. Her brother is a close friend of Luca, so Luca had come for lunch. I just happened to glance when he lifted his tunic to scratch an itch. Hey, that tickles!" The last remark was to Franni, who was measuring from Iulia's armpit to her wrist.

"Poor Luca," Alli sighed. "I *knew* it was him. I just knew it."

"*Poor* Luca? I think you mean rich Luca," Georgia joked. Franni groaned, but Alli and Iulia thought it was hilarious.

Iulia turned serious again. "But we mustn't tell."

"Why?" Franni was picturing all that reward money.

"Well, it's obvious." Alli was doing her big sister know-it-all routine. "If he wanted anyone to know, he would have said something."

"That's right," said Georgia. "I'm sure he just wants the chance to sing Maestro Monteverdi's music." Iulia and Alli nodded. But Franni thought this made no sense. She started measuring Georgia. "If he becomes Duke, he could hire Maestro Monteverdi to write a special show just for him? Couldn't he?"

Iulia let out a haughty laugh. "Honestly, it's a matter of, of . . ."

"Integrity," said Alli.

"Yes, exactly. Integrity."

Franni was still not satisfied. "Shouldn't he want to go back? Isn't it his sacred duty or something, if he was born to be Duke? Wouldn't that be integrity?"

In a harsh voice, Alli sniped, "You never understand anything. You're just too young."

Franni felt her cheeks flush, but she didn't want to start a scene in front of these strangers. Instead of arguing, she slumped down at a table in the corner and tried to focus on getting some work done. There was a dress in front of her that needed repairs to its embroidery. So Franni, sighing deeply, poked the end of a real gold thread through the eye of a needle.

She tried to ignore the older girls, but their chatter was distracting. "We should take a blood oath," Iulia declared.

At that, Franni looked up. Iulia was holding Alli's hand. "We must all swear not to turn Luca in, no matter how much the reward money is."

Georgia skipped over to Franni's table and pulled a pin from a small velvet cushion. "We'll use this to prick our fingers," she said.

Now Franni was truly alarmed. "You can't . . ."

"Shhh!" said all three older girls. Iulia ripped off half a page from Natalias measurement log and scribbled something. "I swear never to tell that Luca is the Duke of Bergamo," she read. She pricked Alli's index finger, then Georgia's, and then her own. They touched the glistening red dots to the paper.

With intense concentration, Iulia folded the paper once, twice, three times. She kissed it, and held it out for Alli and Geogia to kiss. Then she reached up to a wall sconce and set the paper ablaze. Soon all that was left was a curl of ashes floating to the floor.

"Oh, what a beautiful ceremony," said Georgia, holding her hand to her heart.

Franni thought the three of them were crazy, but the blood-bound singers all wiped away tears.

Alli turned dreamily to her friends. "I wonder if we'll have to start calling him Marco instead of Luca."

"He'll always be Luca to me," said Iulia.

Franni couldn't believe what idiots they were. "Surely we'd have to call him 'Your Most Serene Highness.'"

"Not if I'm married to him," Alli answered without hesitation.

"No, *I'm* going to be married to him," said Georgia.

"No, *I* am," insisted Iulia.

A voice from the doorway said, "Perhaps one of you could marry *me* instead." It was Edgardo, blowing kisses to each girl in turn. Only his head was visible behind a table covered in scraps of cloth. Franni was thrilled to see somebody she actually enjoyed talking to. "Ladies," he said, touching the wide brim of his cap. When he bowed, he disappeared completely behind the gold chinz fabric. "Who, may I ask, is the lucky object of your triply glorious affection?"

Franni laughed, delighted, but the other girls pulled their lips back like they'd seen a large insect.

"You ought to be ashamed of yourself, imp," Iulia said, her nose in the air. "Come along, girls. Let's go to rehearsal where the respectable adults are."

"Hope the respectable adults don't mind if you're there with them," Edgardo called as they headed down the hallway. Stepping back into the sewing room, he put his hand to his ear. "Listen carefully, Franni," he quipped, "you can still hear them saying nasty little things to each other."

Franni had a good chuckle. "I thought it was just my sister who acted like that."

"Oh, no, I assure you," said Edgardo. "Most girls turn a bit nasty when they reach a certain age." He looked at her for a few seconds, then gave her a crooked smile. "There are, of course, exceptions."

Franni set down the sleeve she was stitching. "What are you doing here, anyway? I thought you were working on the sets today."

"Indeed I am. But I was told to fetch you. So do come along, if you'd be so kind. Signora Natalia wants you on stage."

"But I'm in the middle of . . ."

"I strongly suggest you obey Signora Natalia. She's worse than a big sister when she's cross." He grinned. "And anyway, you'll get to see the clouds we've been building."

"Clouds?"

"Oh, yes, indeed. I designed the mechanism myself. They move side to side and up and down. And they're big enough for a tenor to sit on." Edgardo trotted out of the room, and Franni followed.

CHAPTER 8

THE REHEARSAL ROOM WAS HUGE, with gorgeous parquet wooden floor and ornate ceiling. *It must be a baquet hall,* Franni thought. But the chaos in there at the moment couldn't have been more different from a gentile royal banquet. There were workmen crawling, climbing, and hammering everywhere, plus bunches of singers and instrumentalists practicing in little groups in every corner.

"Watch your feet, dear," said a man pushing a wide cart into Franni's path. Franni had never seen a cart indoors before. She stepped to the side, trying to figure out what the large round wooden object in the cart might be.

Edgardo must have seen her puzzling over it. "That's part of a pulley system. If we set it up right and draw a rope through it, we can move the clouds around, like I was telling you."

"Ruggiero!" called another man, high up on a scaffold. "Shimmy up here, ya little monkey!"

Edgardo waved back at him. "On my way, Signore."

"Why did he call you Ruggiero?" Franni asked.

"That's my last name. Now, I have to get to work or they'll sack me. Go find Natalia, and I'll see you later on. Okay, Snailnose?"

Franni couldn't help giggling at her new nickname. "Okay." Her smile lingered as she watched Edgardo clamber up the scaffolding. Little monkey was right. She wondered if he'd ever been a sailor.

Morning in the rehearsal hall was like madhouse, and it flew past. Although Franni was kept breathlessly busy taking measurements, mending popped buttons, and fetching fabric, she tried to keep an eye out for Luca. She wanted to observe him, to make a plan for protecting the Duke-in-hiding.

Whenever she could get away with it, Franni glanced over at the end of the room where the clouds were hooked up to the pulleys. A team of men were painting the clouds white and gray. Within an hour, they looked so realistic Franni expected rain to burst from them. Once the clouds were nailed into place, the air rang with commands like "move 'em up," "swing 'em left," and "shoot 'er down faster, if you please." And the clouds moved side to side and up and down, sometimes all the way down to the stage.

The only theater Franni had ever seen was a small traveling troupe that performed in the streets of Verona. They certainly didn't have mechanical clouds. They barely even had scenery.

By lunch break, all she'd decided was that Luca didn't have an especially nice voice. But a duke didn't need to sing, so that didn't matter. Alli, Georgia, and Iulia hung on his every note and swooned at his every glance. He wasn't too bright, either. Once he was even reprimanded by the librettist, Maestro Rinuccini, for singing Alli's lyrics instead of his own. Franni felt like laughing in his face, but Alli just smiled dreamily at him.

I sure hope he likes her too, Franni thought, *or there'll be enough tears to fill Mantua's Lower and Middle Lakes.*

After lunch, Franni learned a lot more about Luca than she wanted to know. She was trying to tie a corset on an overweight contralto by pressing a knee into the woman's back and yanking the laces. It took all of Franni's concentration, and there was a lot of hubbub around her. But a scream and a crash silenced the room. Everyone's attention went to the area being used as the stage. The men and women of the chorus were scattered on either side of Luca. Behind him was one of the huge wooden pulley wheels, split in two. He was surrounded by splinters of white wooden cloud.

"You clumsy half-man!" Luca shrieked upward. Looking down at him from the scaffolding platform, Edgardo had both hands on his head and a horrified expression on his face.

"I'm so very sorry–"

"Don't!" Luca snapped. "Don't you dare apologize. You can never apologize enough. You could have killed me. In fact, I think you were *trying* to kill me."

Edgardo shook his head frantically. "I assure you–"

"Well, I can assure you, you tiny monstrosity, your kind will bring this production bad luck." Luca spun to face Maestro Monteverdi, who was massaging his temples with his long fingers. "Maestro, cast this man out onto the street. Surely you can find another builder to replace him."

Everyone turned to see what Monteverdi would do. Franni prayed as fast as she could that Edgardo would not lose his job or be sent to prison. "He didn't do it on purpose!" A hundred gasps surprised her. She was horrified to realize she'd said those words aloud. She clapped her hand over her mouth.

Franni held her breath and said a silent prayer to protect Edgardo from being fired. Maestro Monteverdi daubed his brow with a kerchief. He looked even more exhausted and sad than usual. "I think–" he said, and paused to think. "I think we have already lost enough valuable members of this company to the smallpox." Franni breathed out in relief. "And I think," the Maestro bent slightly to look straight into Luca's eye, "that you are a mere chorus boy, who has less skill than that engineer Signore Ruggiero, whom you call a 'half-man.' Obviously you have no experience in the theater. If you did, you would know that these scenery mechanisms go wrong all the time."

"Indeed, indeed," sighed Signore Striggio. Signore Rinuccini nodded vigorously.

Monteverdi continued, "Yet, for this production, our Most Serene Highness wants more complicated mechanisms than have ever been used in the theater. They are bound to malfunction in rehearsal."

"Most certainly true," Rinuccini agreed.

"Therefore, no one is to blame. It seems to be the will of the Almighty that theater rehearsals be marred by falling debris. On the other hand," he said in a growing voice, "it is pure human weakness to sing out of tune and with the wrong rhythm, as you insist on doing, boy. I suggest you sing in better tune and with brighter rhythm, or it is you who shall be replaced."

There was an undertone of murmurs in the crowd. The lute player guffawed. Guiseppe held his violin in front of his mouth. But Maestro Monteverdi was not in a jovial mood. "Back to work, all of you!" he roared. "This is the most undisciplined company I've ever had the misfortune to be saddled with. If your performance of *Arianna* doesn't make me lose my post as Maestro di Cappella, it will be a miracle."

The threatening attitude seemed to be catching. "Seamstresses!" bayed Natalia. "Heads back in your duties, girls. There's measuring and hemming aplenty. Back to the sewing room, all of you."

Franni forced herself to focus on her work. But her mind kept going over and over how awfully Luca had treated Edgardo. And the more she thought about it, the more she realized that this was the final proof. Luca had spoken like a nobleman to a commoner. He was definitely the Duke of Bergamo.

When the singers were finally dismissed at the end of the day, Alli met Franni outside the sewing room and whispered to her urgently. "You have to swear."

"Swear what?"

"That you won't tell. About you-know-who. You didn't take the blood oath."

Franni shrugged, examining her sister's face.

Tears welled up in Alli's eyes. She whispered so softly, she was practically just mouthing the words. "Promise you won't tell. It's not what Luca wants, and I can't bear the thought of him being unhappy. Please, Franni."

So Franni agreed. What could she do? On the one hand, Luca had insulted her friend. But Alli was all the family she had left in the world, apart from her famous uncle in Brescia she'd only heard about, never met. That didn't count. She put her right hand over her heart and made a reluctant promise. "Fine. I won't tell. But I get the rest of the night off from hearing about that stupid boy."

"*Fine,*" Alli snapped. "I'm walking home with Iulia instead of you. How do you like *that*?"

"*Fine.*" Franni pushed her sister down the hallway and closed herself in the sewing room.

After all the musicians and crew had departed, Natalia gave Franni a pile of silver-embroidered green cloth to fold. "And then you may go," Natalia said. She left, probably to work for a few more hours. Franni had a feeling she never got to rest.

Edgardo entered the sewing room, a wig in his hand.

"Hey," said Franni, embarrassed for what he'd been through earlier.

"Hey-ho Franni-o," he sang, not seeming upset in the least. "Aren't you walking home with your sister?"

Franni shook her head and rolled her eyes. "No way. Alli's just impossible to be around."

"Just wants to talk about boys, I'll bet." He picked up a sheaf of horsehairs and pulled one out.

"Mainly that stupid Duke of Bergamo."

Edgardo leaned closer to his work, threading the horsehair into a bald area on the wig. "Ah-hah. The famous Duke of Bergamo. That does seem to be a popular topic these days."

Franni set down the luxurious green fabric and rested her elbows on it. "Shouldn't the Duke, whoever he is, just go and be a duke? Isn't that his duty?" She didn't want to give away too much, but she was anxious to talk about this with someone who wasn't a love-sick teen girl.

Setting down the wig, Edgardo asked, "What do you mean, his duty?"

"Well, isn't it in his blood? Isn't that the whole point of these men wandering around Italy looking for exactly this guy? Because his bloodlines say he's the Duke?"

Edgardo's face was earnest. "And what about his freedoms? His rights?"

"What do you mean?"

"What if he doesn't want to be the Duke? What if he wants to be . . ."

"A singer!" Franni gasped at her loose tongue. "Or something."

"Sure. A singer or something. Instead of a duke. It's a person's life we're talking about, you know."

Franni wasn't sure how to respond. Her brain was swirling, but she couldn't quite form an argument. "Edgardo, would you walk me home? You're more interesting to talk to than stuffy old Natalia."

"It would be an honor, Snailnose," said Edgardo. He put the long, white-blond wig on his head for a moment and batted his eyelashes. Then he dropped the wig on the table and jogged around the table on his little legs. "I'll even buy you some roasted almonds from Mr. Peniero's stand."

"Oh, thanks!"

"But Franni?"

She turned, and that earnest look was back on his face. "There's something else you should understand about this Duke business."

"Really, it doesn't matter to me. It's just Alli is . . ."

"It's very dangerous."

Franni felt a chill along her back. "Dangerous? How?"

Before answering, Edgardo popped his head out into the hallway and looked in both directions. When he spoke, it was in a hushed tone. "Two reasons. First, the reward money. Some people will do anything to get money. Second, what's at stake in the town that's missing its duke."

"Bergamo."

"Right. Bergamo. Dreadful place, I understand. Anyway, there could be people—bad people—who want to lay claim to the dukedom. They'll be the most dangerous of all."

Suddenly, Franni was absolutely sure of something. She needed Edgardo's help protecting Luca. She hadn't realized how much danger he might be in. And if he was in danger, then so was Alli because she was always around him. It was worth breaking her promise to her sister if it would keep her safe.

Bending down, Franni whispered in Edgardo's ear. "Luca, that boy who was so mean to you. He's the Duke."

A hint of sarcasm glinted in his eye. "You don't say."

Franni gasped. "You *knew*?"

"Well, let's just say I guessed, like you did."

"Oh, but it's definitely true."

"And how can you be sure, my lovely Franni?"

"Iulia saw the birthmark."

At that, a laugh exploded through Edgardo's nose. His hand gripped the wall, as if he'd fall over from sheer amusement if he let go. "Now, that's a story I'd like to hear someday."

"It's not funny."

He sobered up. "No. Not funny."

"He's in danger."

"Right."

Franni started feeling desperate and she spoke faster and faster. "And my sister's in love with him, so I'm afraid, and we can't tell anyone, but I couldn't bear it if anything happened to Alli, she's my only sister and I'd never forgive myself and neither would my parents watching from above and oh, oh, Edgardo, please. You have to help me protect Luca from all those bad people. But it has to be a secret."

"All right, then."

"All right, then?"

"I'll help you."

Franni couldn't believe it. "Even after how he treated you today?"

Edgardo snickered as he led her toward the nearest servant's exit. "My dearest Francesca, in my vast experience of life, I've learned that two things are certain in this world."

They stepped out into the evening air. Franni breathed in the warm breeze, scented with new spring blossoms. "What's certain in this world, Edgardo?"

"First, that normal people will mistreat dwarves. Second, that nobles will mistreat the lower classes. I suffered the brunt of both of those facts this morning. But never mind. That's how life goes. If this is important to you,

I'll do it. I don't have many friends, so I try to help those I do have. We're friends, are we not?"

Franni liked the sound of that. "Oh, yes, Edgardo."

"Then I'll keep your secret."

"And you'll help me protect, um, *that person* from being forced back to, um, that particular place?"

"Or worse. Yes, I'll help. Now, come on. Let's find you those roasted almonds and get you home. We've both had a very long day."

CHAPTER 9

EVERY DAY, THE PEOPLE WORKING on *Arianna* labored as if they were building a massive stone castle. With only two weeks until the performance, there was a sense of mild panic that lay like a fog over the whole enterprise. But Franni, who was only responsible for sewing hems and buttons, wasn't nervous. And while she might have been sick of the costumes, she loved to look at the scenery and hear the music. At every chance, Franni sneaked out of the sewing room to watch rehearsal from behind the sets.

There was a huge crew working on the scenery. "It's already over a hundred men," Natalia said one day when they found the lunch buffet wiped clean by hungry construction workers. "By the performance at the end of May, I'm told it will be nearly three times that." She wrinkled her nose. "Imagine how they'll get underfoot when we're trying to help with costume changes or repair ripped seams at lightning speed!"

Franni didn't dare to believe she'd heard correctly. "You mean we'll actually be backstage? During the performance?"

Natalia tossed off her reply. "Well, of course. What did you expect?" Then she hurried across the room to handle an emergency with the buttons on a pudgy singer's vest.

Franni stood there, imagining the confusion and excitement of making the performance happen. It would have been thrilling enough for any old show. She certainly had never dreamed of being in the celebration of a Duke's family wedding. True, she would be one of thousands, but it was still a lot to take in.

"You okay, Snailnose?" Franni jumped when Edgardo poked her playfully in the ribs. "You look as if someone just gave you a mountain of candy and you're not sure which piece to eat first."

"Oh, don't say that," Franni laughed, pointing to the empty platters on the table. "I'm already so hungry."

"You poor thing. Let's fix that." Edgardo motioned for Franni to follow. "As it happens, I have a private stash." He led the way down the hall to a large room where spare lumber, paints, and old sets were stored. There was a pungent smell of sawdust.

Edgardo lit a torch and picked his way to the back of the room. "Hold this, please." He handed Franni a torch and used both hands to remove the woven lid from a round basket, taller than he was. "Hope the mice haven't found it yet."

"What is it?" Franni stood on tiptoe.

"Hey, keep that light still!" Edgardo pulled the basket onto its side and crawled in head first. His voice came out muffled. "It's still here, and I don't think there are any bite marks."

Franni laughed at the sight of Edgardo's feet sticking out of the basket. "You know, I used to have a puppy who knocked over baskets and hid in them. Are you part puppy, Edgardo?"

Squirming, Edgardo backed out and looked up into the torchlight. "I've been called worse," he said with a sad smile. In his hands was a cloth-covered bundle, which he held up toward Franni. "Bread?"

He unwrapped a large, round loaf with one wedge cut out of it. Edgardo sawed off a piece for each of them with the knife he carried in his pocket. He found a prop vase to hold the torch. It was the most perfect picnic Franni could remember, and the most delicious bread, too.

"Mmm." Sitting on a wooden beam nailed across the back of an old stage set, Franni swung her legs forward and back. She tried to talk, but had just stuffed her mouth full of the rich, sweet bread.

"Take your time," said Edgardo. "I'm a very patient man."

The moment she'd swallowed, Franni gushed, "This is wonderful. Where did you get it?"

Edgardo gave her a sly smile. "I made it, as a matter of fact."

This news made Franni cough on a crumb.

Edgardo tapped her on the back. "Is it really so surprising I can bake bread?" He jumped down and pulled a jug of wine and a metal cup from the basket. "Drink this."

Gulping a mouthful of liquid to get her pipes back in order, Franni shook her head. "No, it's just that you're so talented. You can do so many things: make wigs, build mechanical clouds, and now bake the tastiest bread ever."

Edgardo gave Franni a little bow. "And don't forget about my incredible charm and wit."

Groaning, Franni said, "Oh, yes. That, too." She took another bite and chewed more carefully. "So, how did you learn to do all these things?"

Edgardo wrapped up the remaining bread and corked the wine. It wasn't until he'd righted the tall basket and fitted on its lid that he answered. "I've needed to learn all kinds of skills." He turned to Franni and she could see how serious his face had become. "I've just had that sort of life. Here, let me help you down. We should get back to work before they come looking for us."

When he stretched out his arms Franni grabbed them to steady herself. Without a word or a smile, Edgardo picked up the torch and guided them through the debris to the door. Franni's heart ached to see the change in her friend's disposition. Before she stepped out into the corridor, she whispered, "Please forgive me if I said something to hurt your feelings."

Edgardo took one of her hands in both of his. "I assure you, Snailnose, it is Fortune that's hurt my feelings, not you. Never you. Your friendship brings me nothing but happiness."

Relieved, Franni practically skipped back to the rehearsal room. She didn't even mind when Natalia jumped down her throat for disappearing. The knowledge that she had a true friend made Franni's work seem light. The afternoon was flying by quickly when Franni overheard a conversation between two women from the chorus.

She was standing near these women, taking notes for Natalia as she called out measurements for a huge crimson cloth. The cloth was supposed to be draped over the royal carriage of King Theseus in the opera. Franni couldn't understand why they didn't simply use a huge piece of material, rather than measure it exactly. Therefore, she wasn't paying very close attention, and the conversation nearby drew her ear.

"Do you think it's him?" said a woman in a gray dress. Her corset was pulling her chest and stomach into a completely flat surface, in the latest style. Franni couldn't imagine how this woman could sing. The other woman, whom Franni remembered for her suspiciously blond hair, nodded. "I'm telling you, I just happened to see his birthmark earlier when he was trying on his costume for Act III."

"Are you getting these numbers down?" Natalie barked, shaking Franni from her eavesropping.

"Yes, Signora," she said, trying to sound obedient. Not wanting to get fired, Franni tried to concentrate. But all she could think about was which Act III costume fittings they'd done that morning. There were too many costumes, and she couldn't remember. Hoping for a clue, she scanned the rehearsal room.

In the far corner was the beautiful Margharita Romano, a soprano from the court of Florence who'd come to Mantua just to play the goddess Venus. She had tried on her blue and gold robes right before lunch. Franni was sure about that. Madame Romano was so slender that Natalia had made a crack about how Venus should look more like a woman than a boy. Fortunately, Madame Romano had taken the insult in good humor.

I wish she were the Duke, thought Franni. *At least she has a nice personality.*

Automatically, her eyes scanned the room for Luca. There he was, hand on hip, holding forth with some bragging speech. Alli, Iulia, and several other woman sat at his feet. Franni's curiosity burned. "Signora Natalia," she said, helping her boss fold the giant red drapery, "was there a fitting for the men's chorus this morning?"

Natalia looked up sharply, so Franni invented a reason for her question. "I'm just making sure the Act III clothes are measured, since they need all those silk leaves sewn on."

Immediately, Natalia's face relaxed. "I had Donata measure the boys today, yes. Thanks for thinking of it, dear. You'll start sewing on leaves tomorrow."

Franni forced herself to grin. "Yes, Signora." Her fingers ached just thinking about all those silk leaves.

So, those gossiping women probably had seen Luca after all. Why was he being so careless? Did he not know he was the Duke? If he did know, did he not realize he might be in danger? Or could he be such a braggart that he *wanted* to show off that birthmark?

The only thing Franni knew for sure was that she needed to discuss this with someone she trusted. Edgardo was nowhere in sight, so Alli would have to do. "Maybe she can talk some sense into that idiot Luca," she said to herself. She waved at Alli and beckoned for her to join her behind a huge ship on one side of the room. The ship was actually a flat wooden prop, with ropes attached in the back to make it look like it was sailing.

"What do you want?" Alli snapped. She seemed distracted. "Oh, listen to *that.*" Alli held one hand up to silence Franni and the other to her heart. A tenor voice, pure as liquid silver, flowed through the air. "Isn't Rasi just heavenly?"

"Who?" Franni was impatient to say what was on her mind. "Who's Rasi?"

Alli gasped. "Francesco Rasi, only one of the greatest tenors in Italy. This isn't just about costumes, you know. There are singers in the costumes. Rasi is playing King Theseus."

Franni was not finding this very interesting. "Who's King Theseus?"

"The husband of Arianna, of course." Alli said it as if every single person on the earth except Franni already knew that.

Breathing deeply to control her temper, Franni tried again. "Yeah, he sounds great. I wanted to tell you something. I think Luca–"

"I should play the role of Arianna," moaned Alli, plowing right through Franni's words. "Luca says they're planning to give the role to someone much too old. She's *thirty,* Luca says." Alli whispered frantically. "Luca says he can use his influence, Franni. You know, his *influence.* Maybe he can get me an audition to sing Arianna. So you have to help me steal the music."

"What?" Franni thought she must have misheard.

"The music for Arianna's part. I have to steal a copy, so I'm ready when Luca gets me an audition."

"Have you lost your mind?" Completely forgetting the reason she'd wanted to speak to Alli in the first place, Franni held up her hands and shook her head. "I'm not stealing anything for anybody."

Alli's face grew dark, and Franni knew a big fight was coming. But the girls were interrupted by a commotion in the rehearsal room. Alli peeked out from behind the ship and asked a man from the crew, "What's happening?"

He answered, "It's the Duke."

So, the search was over. Franni froze, waiting to hear Luca's name. Instead, a deep, polished voice announced, "Make way for his Most Serene Highness, Duke Vincenzo Gonzaga."

Oh, thought Franni, *the Duke of Mantua!*

A trumpet blared, much too loud for the indoor space. Franni watched as everyone, from Maestro Monteverdi and his star tenor down to the lowest servant, dropped to a deep bow or curtsy. Too busy watching everyone else to think how to behave herself, Franni stayed upright. So she saw the entrance of Duke Gonzaga. He was surrounded by six guards, three in front and three behind. He wore a silk outfit the color of a summer peach. Franni had never seen such luxurious material.

"*Franni!*" Alli hissed, and Franni finally realized she had better curtsy.

She did so just in time. As she bowed her head and bent her knees, the Duke strode near her. Franni got a close look at his shoes, which were made from tapestry that seemed to have a hundred colors of thread. *It must have taken someone six months to make that one pair,* Franni thought.

"Good Maestro Monteverdi," the Duke said. "Attend, if you please."

Monteverdi came forward and lunged into an acrobatic bow, one leg stretched far forward. "Your most humble servant, Serene Excellency," said the composer.

"We have decided to grant your petition to award the role of your little wedding entertainment to Madame Andreini."

Franni heard Alli gasp lightly.

Monteverdi bowed again. "I am most deeply grateful for your Highness's boundless generosity and wisdom."

"Right. That is all. Carry on." The Duke turned and strode out, followed by his guards and his trumpet player.

Everyone stood and started whispering. Looking around, Franni was amused at how everyone was reacting. It was as if this were a matter of war and peace, or starvation, or flood. As her eyes ran across the room, they stopped on something that gave her an icy chill. For one second, one terrifying second, she thought she saw that face again. That long, craggy face with crooked eyes. It was burnt into her memory, that man she'd seen lurking near the Palazzo the first time she'd come there.

Franni caught her breath and closed her eyes. When she opened them again, the face was gone.

CHAPTER 10

THOSE CROOKED FEATURES STRUCK such fear in Franni's chest, all she could think about was finding a friendly face. "Have you seen Edgardo?" she asked one set-builder after another. They all shook their heads. Some of them snickered about how "the daft little girl's in love with the doll-sized man."

Franni's cheeks felt hot, and tears blurred her vision. She didn't even recognize Natalia for a moment when the head seamstress handed Franni a piece of paper.

"Are you sleepwalking, girl?" Natalia seemed harried. "Look, I normally wouldn't ask this of you, but Donata has a pile of work and two of my other girls have been taken ill. I need you to start this dress for me."

Franni tried to focus on the paper, which showed a drawing of a dress with an attached apron. There was a list of measurements below the sketch. Terrified of this responsibility, Franni shook her head. "Signora Natalia, I'm not sure I can do this."

Natalia's face softened and she spoke more gently than usual. "Just work on the apron. You made me a very nice apron when you first arrived."

"Thank you, Signora."

"There's a bolt of lemon-yellow linen on the back right table in the sewing room. That will do nicely. Off you go."

Taking one last hopeful glance around for Edgardo—and a frightened check for the crooked-eyed man—Franni headed out the rehearsal room door. It was in the hallway that she found Edgardo, shuffling toward her. As short as his legs were, that seemed to be as close as he could come to running.

"They're coming!" he sputtered as he waddled by, not slowing down to talk to her.

"Who?" Franni asked.

He reached back to grab Franni's wrist and paused just long enough to whisper, "The guards from Bergamo. Don't know if they've heard about Luca, or if they're just searching everywhere. But we don't want to take that chance."

Franni looked from Edgardo to the dress instructions, now crumpled in her hand. She had to help that stupid Luca for Alli's sake. "Okay. I'll hide Luca. You stall the guards. Put them off the scent."

"How should I do that, pray?"

Franni took Edgardo by the shoulders and spoke close to his face. She tried to give him the courage she didn't feel. "Make something up. You seem to have all this wild, adventurous life experience. Use it." Not waiting for his response, Franni dodged past him, back into the rehearsal room.

Luca, standing tall with his shoulders back, was easy to spot. "Gotta come with me for a fitting," Franni said, tugging at his sleeve. "Right away."

He just looked at her like she was a bug crawling up his arm, so she decided to make use of his vanity. "Your Act III tunic is all wrong. You'll look like an old beggarman if you wear it like this. Last chance to fix it." Seeing a glint of worry in his eyes, Franni turned and trotted off. As she'd hoped, Luca followed her.

She could hear Edgardo's voice down the hall. After she opened the sewing room door and pushed Luca in, she saw Edgardo bowing before a team of guards in the red and black silk uniforms of Bergamo. "Wait in there," she ordered Luca firmly, and closed him in the sewing room. Franni lifted her skirts and darted closer to Edgardo and the guards, keeping close to the wall. In a safe position behind a pillar, Franni looked forward to hearing whatever amazing story Edgardo would confuse them with.

And confused was exactly how the guards looked. “Are you sure it was the Viceroy?” the tallest guard asked, bending his knees to talk to Edgardo.

Edgardo shrugged and waved his hand. “How would I know? He just said his name was Bertoletti, and that he was sent by someone named Ararro.”

At that second name, all the guards gasped and exchanged glances.

“But why didn’t he stay and speak directly to us?” asked another guard.

Edgardo opened his palms toward the ceiling. “What am I, a sorcerer? Who can tell why one man does something? This Bertoletti, he seemed to be in a hurry. He mentioned needing to ride after another set of guards.”

“The ones who went to Verona?”

Hearing the name of her own town, Franni felt a pang of homesickness that nearly made her cry out.

“All I know is what I told you,” said Edgardo. “Venice is calling off the search. I guess they found another heir for Bergamo.”

“Is it really so surprising? You’re not here in the Palazzo looking for anyone in particular, are you? You’re just hoping you’ll get lucky and find him. Right?”

Two of the guards shuffled the feet and shrugged, but one of them stepped forward. “This is none of your affair. And anyway, I don’t believe you. Get out of our way so we can keep searching.” This guard had such broad shoulders, he seemed to be as wide as Edgardo was tall.

Franni feared for her friend’s safety, but Edgardo still spoke breezily. “Suit yourself. But, if Ararro has called off the search and you don’t go back home, do you know what that means?” He stopped there. The guards leaned forward, obviously curious. Franni peeked an inch farther from behind her pillar, as curious as the guards.

Finally, the tallest guard seemed to figure out the puzzle. “It means we won’t get paid.” He spat on the polished marble floor. “Come on, boys. We’re wasting our time. Have been since the day we left Bergamo.” The broad-shouldered guard made a grunting sound as if he didn't approve, but he followed when the others turned to go. The tall guard tossed a coin to Edgardo, who clutched it in his fist and bowed deeply. The guards turned and tromped down the hallway, their armor clanging.

Franni had the urge to applaud her friend's impressive performance, but she was also spilling over with questions. As soon as the guards were out of sight, she leapt out from behind her pillar.

"Ahh!" yelped Edgardo. "You could kill a fellow that way!"

"Sorry," Franni giggled, "but you were just great. How did you know the right names to use, to convince them?"

Edgardo grinned. "The Republic of Venice is run by swine. However, they're very amusing swine. I've watched their entertainments closely since I was young. And I've seen many a stout lad tremble at the name of Ararro, the Viceroy. He's famous for being nasty to people who disobey him."

"Edgardo, you're amazing."

Looking up at Franni, Edgardo waggled his eyebrows. "You know, you may be right."

"Hey, Ruggiero," said a voice behind Franni. It was the set foreman. "Get yourself in that rehearsal room, or I'll dock your pay."

"The Amazing Edgardo is called to duty, my friend." He bowed slightly and hurried off with his strange shuffling run.

Franni remembered that she had an apron to sew. Plus, she needed to figure out what to tell Luca. He was still waiting in the sewing room to be fitted for a tunic that actually fit him just fine. She was still puzzling over this problem as she opened the sewing room door. But instead of Luca, she found Alli and Iulia there. They were in the middle of a big fight.

"He does not," said Alli.

"He does, too," countered Iulia. She bared her teeth like a mountain lion.

Franni didn't have time for this. She had a duke to protect. "Where's Luca?" she demanded.

Donata was working at one of the tables. "Maestro Monteverdi called for the men's chorus rehearsal."

Alli complained, "I came in here to fetch Luca so he wouldn't miss rehearsal and get in trouble. I thought he was in here with you, Franni. But what do I find instead?" Alli slammed her hand down on the table, making Donata jump mid-stitch. "I find him kissing my so-called friend Iulia."

Franni huffed. "Come on, you two. Shouldn't you be at rehearsal, too?" She was relieved to hear Luca was accounted for, but she wasn't in the mood to listen to older girls fighting over a boy. "I have an apron to make, if you don't mind."

Donata pointed to the lemon-yellow linen, and Franni spread it over the table next to hers. She looked up at her sister. "Can't you two tell that Luca's a creep? He flirts with every girl in the company."

"That's not true," Alli whined.

"He's gorgeous and sweet," gushed Iulia.

That comment made Alli turn and lash out at her friend again. "You're not allowed to say that about my Luca."

"*Your* Luca?"

"Yes. Mine. He likes me best."

Franni glanced helplessly at Donata, who winked and smiled, making deep wrinkles in her old face. Franni measured out the front of the apron while her sister and Iulia bickered.

"Does he really like you best?" Iulia sneered. "You saw him kissing me."

"Because he asked me to marry him!" Alli shouted.

Donata squealed and sucked the finger she'd just pricked. Franni noticed that she'd lost control of her scissors and sliced through the apron's front. "He *what*?"

Alli swaggered toward her. "He told me he could get me the part of Arianna if I agreed to marry him."

Although Franni knew there was no point in reasoning with her love-struck sister, she had to try anyway. "Duke Gonzaga said that Madame Andreini is playing Arianna."

"But Luca promised me. And I believe him. Because of—" She glanced significantly at Donata, then back at Franni. "Well, you know why he'd be able to."

Iulia's eyes were glassy. Her cheeks were gray. "He never could've said that to you."

"Well, he did." Alli curled a ringlet of hair around her finger. "Just this morning."

"You're lying!" Iulia wailed.

Franni thought it was time to find out just how duke-crazy her sister was. "And you're not actually planning to marry him just for a stupid singing part, right?"

"Of course I'll marry him," said Alli, staring hard at Iulia. "I'll be Arianna, *and* I'll be a–" she mouthed the next word, "duchess."

A strangled scream came through Iulia's clenched teeth. "You're not the only one who can play dirty," she panted. "I've got powerful friends, too. You'll never get the part of Arianna, but I *will* get the solo in Act II."

Alli looked alarmed. "Steffi Baragna's singing that solo."

Iulia cackled. "Steffi's got the fever. The Maestro needs a replacement. And it's going to be me. Just you watch!" Iulia stormed out. Alli stormed out after her.

Franni started to follow, but looked down at the ruined apron in her hands.

"You go ahead, dear," said Donata. "I'll take care of the dress. These fingers are old, but they're still mighty nimble."

"Oh, thanks, Donata. You're so sweet." Franni brought her the fabric and the sheet of measurements. Then she kissed her on each cheek.

"Not at all. You run along quick, quick, and keep those hot-blooded girls from plucking out each other's eyes."

Franni was actually more worried about them plucking out the Duke of Bergamo's eyes. She hurried out into the hallway and down to the rehearsal room. When she entered, she didn't hear the usual chaotic pounding and grinding of the set builders, chattering of singers, or playing of instruments. Instead, the only sound was Maestro Monteverdi's voice. He was towering over Iulia as many of the cast members watched.

"And why should I care that your father knows the husband of Madame Andreini?" the Maestro was saying.

Iulia's voice shook. "Well, Maestro, I just thought that, out of respect for the Andreini family, you would grant me a favor."

The composer stood to his full height, which was far taller than the soprano. "Favor? What favor?"

Iulia cleared her throat. "Well, Maestro, you see, I—"

"Speak up. I'm a very busy man." He indicated the hundred people around him.

Taking a big breath, Iulia spoke loudly and quickly, as if she were afraid she might forget the words of her speech. "I heard Steffi Baragna is ill, and you need someone to sing the serving maid's solo in Act II, and I thought you might give me that chance." There were several gasps around the room. Iulia added, "If it please you, Maestro."

Monteverdi folded his arms, which Franni thought made the slender man look like an insect. "It does not please me," he said. There were more gasps around the room. Everyone hung on each detail as if they were watching a wrestling match. "And, do you know why it does not please me, Signorina Sparzi?"

Iulia shook her head, clearly wishing she could turn to dust. Franni noticed she was biting her lip, trying not to cry.

"Do you imagine it is because I don't respect your father? Giovanni Sparzi's work on the stage is well known to me." Iulia looked up hopefully. But the composer growled at her. "So, your father is an actor. What does that have to do with you singing my music?"

Iulia dropped her eyes and shrugged.

"Nothing!" Monteverdi spat out the word. "All that matters is the music, and how it conveys the words. And you do not sing well enough to take the solo in Act II."

Even Franni gasped at that harsh pronouncement. Iulia made a choking sound and slapped a hand over her mouth.

"You!" Maestro Monteverdi called to someone behind Iulia. Everyone looked around, not sure who he meant. "The sandy-blond one. Ategnati's niece." Franni's heart stopped. He meant Alli! "You, girl." Alli stepped forward and curtsied. "Your voice is sweet and your rhythm clear and sure. Friday morning you will try to sing the solo in Act II. See Signore Striggio for the music to practice."

Franni didn't hear what Alli said to the Maestro because she was too busy cheering. Iulia, tears pouring down her red face, elbowed past her violently and ran out the door.

"Settle down, company," shouted Striggio. "Perhaps you are aware that we have a command performance to give in a mere two weeks. Perhaps you will recall that several noble, even royal, families will be in attendance at this performance. And perhaps it has not escaped you that this production looks and sounds more like an afternoon in a barnyard than a Duke's wedding." There were a few nervous titters. "So, let's get to work, shall we?"

For the rest of the day, Franni helped Donata sew the new dress. It was a huge project, so time flew by. Before Franni realized the time, Alli showed up to say that rehearsal was over.

Because she was so proud of her sister for getting the solo, Franni managed to put Alli's silly comments about marrying Luca out of her mind. Alli, of course, was in an excellent mood. On the way home, she bought Franni a bracelet made of little wooden beads from a vendor near the Palazzo. And she pointed out the early moon, just as she'd always done in happier days in Verona.

By the time the girls reached Maria's boarding house, Franni had forgotten there'd been any unpleasantness that afternoon. They could smell roasted fish and spring vegetables as they approached the door, and Franni felt the most contented she had in a long time.

Flashing a smile at Alli, hungry Franni ran through the doorway toward the fragrant food. But in the foyer she crashed into Iulia. Her eyes were still red. Strands of her hair stuck out in every direction.

"You'll pay," Iulia whispered hoarsely. "You'll both pay."

"What do you mean?" demanded Alli, stepping in behind Franni. "Iulia, what have you done?"

Iulia sneered and shook her head. "You'll just have to wait and see. But, trust me, you'll pay, and so will that louse, Luca." She spun around and disappeared up the stairs. Franni felt a chill down her back.

CHAPTER 11

FEARING WHAT SHE MIGHT FIND waiting for her at work the next morning, Franni spent a jumpy night. "What do you think Iulia's planning?" she asked Alli over and over.

But Alli would only snort and say, "Nothing. I've told you a hundred times. What can she possibly do?"

There was nothing she could do to stop Friday morning from arriving. Franni held her breath as she entered the Palazzo. She tried to prepare herself for anything. But nothing strange happened. No scary people pounced out of cupboards at her. Nobody was poisoned by the lunch buffet or struck by falling scenery.

Soon Franni was swept up in the swirl of the workday, hemming costumes, running measurements and piles of fabric back and forth from room to room, helping with fittings. Even the members of the orchestra needed special coats and trousers made, with lace trailing off the sleeves.

"I can't play with all this frou-frou flopping around," complained the stick-shaped man who played theorbo.

Giuseppe Ruffo told her, "This jacket makes an annoying crackling sound when I draw my bow across the strings. Could you take off some of the beads?"

"The collar's in the way of the fingerboard," claimed the bass-viol player. That was right before the man who played the portative organ said he'd run his stocking on the wooden leg of his instrument.

It became Franni's job to take notes and watch for problems as the musicians played. She marked down if any part of the costumes got caught in instruments or under fingers as they pressed keys, covered holes, and plucked strings. She hadn't realized it was possible to be so busy.

The week flew by, each day more of a whirlwind than the last. Franni started to enjoy Maestro Monteverdi's music, now that the orchestra and singers really knew their parts. She loved how sometimes the orchestra would start to repeat a note faster and faster. That always happened when the singers had very dramatic lyrics. Maestro called it the "excited style," and it did make Franni's heart pound. She felt like she was sharing the character's emotions.

"Nobody else can write songs so true to how people feel," sighed Alli. She and Franni wiped tears from their eyes one morning after King Theseus, played by Mr. Rasi, sang about how much he loved Arianna. "Too bad Arianna's heart gets broken," she added, sighing again.

Franni was confused. "Her heart gets broken? I thought Theseus was her husband. And didn't he just sing a love song about her?"

Alli rolled her eyes in that way big sisters are expert at. "Honestly, Franni, don't you know anything?"

"So *tell* me, if it's really that important."

Perching on the edge of King Theseus's throne, which was in the corner while it wasn't needed, Alli explained. "After Arianna saves his life and runs away with him, Theseus decides he can find a better queen."

"That's mean." Franni wanted to say something about Luca at this point, but she knew the fight that would cause.

"It gets worse. Theseus abandons her on a deserted island."

"*What*?"

"Yes, and poor Arianna thinks she's going to die alone in this scary place."

"No!"

"But along comes Dionysus."

Franni repeated the unusual name. "Di-o-ny-sus? Who's that?"

"He's the god of wine. And he falls in love with Arianna."

Franni was delighted by Arianna's good fortune. "So, she gets to marry a god? That's amazing!" She worried about the starry look in Alli's eyes. Her sister was thinking about that idiot Luca again, as if he were her own personal god of wine.

* * *

Knowing the story of *Arianna* helped Franni appreciate the costumes she was working on. One afternoon Natalia told her to sew strips of burgundy velvet to the hem of Dionysus's long jacket. "That's the color of wine," Franni explained to old Donata. "Dionysus is the god of wine, you know."

But enjoying her work didn't keep Franni from feeling lonely in the sewing room. Donata rarely had anything to say besides, "Mmm-hmm." She spent all her time bent over her work. And Alli was always either rehearsing, mooning over Luca, or gossiping with Georgia about Iulia. She was no fun.

Franni's only true friend was Edgardo. When they could slip away to the props storage room, he shared his fresh-baked bread with her. He told her amusing stories of all the places he'd been (or pretended he'd been, or imagined he'd been—Franni couldn't tell which).

Best of all, one day he taught her how to operate the wonderful mechanical cloud. It was an athletic event for Franni to climb that scaffolding in all her skirts and petticoats. But she was determined, and Edgardo helped as much as he could without being impolite.

Once they'd reached the top, he invited Franni to sit on the rickety platform. "This lever," he said, pointing, "turns this spool of rope." Bracing his feet, Edgardo grabbed the crank handle with his stubby fingers. "Cranking forward lifts the cloud." He heaved into the crank like a sailor raising a mainsail. When Franni peeked over the edge, she could see the top of the wooden cloud rising toward her.

"Oh, look!" she exclaimed. "May I lower it?"

His hands still tight around the crank, Edgardo studied Franni. She prepared herself for the word *no*, but instead Edgardo smiled and said, "How about you help me lower it? Come opposite me here."

Delighted for the chance to pitch in, Franni braced herself on the scaffolding, facing the crank on the other side. When Edgardo removed one of his hands, Franni wrapped both of hers around the crank. They turned it slowly. The ropes fed through the pulleys, and the cloud gradually dropped to the stage. Although her arm muscles burned, Franni didn't stop until a crew worker below had signaled that the cloud was stable.

"That was fun!" she said. "I'd love to make something like that." She'd meant it as a hint, hoping Edgardo would teach her more about how it worked. But he just smiled and looked off into the distance, as if he were remembering real clouds in a far-away sky.

* * *

By the end of the week, Franni had forgotten Iulia's threats. And another exciting topic had replaced the Duke of Bergamo in the gossip at Maria's boarding house.

"Are they really arriving today?" Georgia asked at breakfast on Friday. Alli nodded.

Maria placed a bowl of porridge in front of each tenant. Franni would have preferred bread and cheese, but Maria believed hot porridge kept her girls healthy. "Who's arriving today?" Maria asked.

"Caccini's women," many of them answered together. Even Franni said it, although she didn't quite understand who they were.

"And why does this Caccini have so many women?" Maria's question drew a laugh.

Alli explained. "Giulio Caccini is a composer and music maestro in Florence. And he trained a special group of women to sing for the Duke there."

Maria stopped pouring water into Georgia's glass and looked up. "Why would we need them in Mantua?" She moved her hand in a big arc to indicate everyone at the table. "There are plenty of fine singers here already."

The tenants blushed and giggled at the compliment but quieted down when Iulia stepped into the doorway. "Maestro Monteverdi doesn't think we're good enough," she growled. "He thinks we need these Florentines in the chorus to make it better. Wouldn't want precious Maestro to embarrass himself in front of all those noble guests!"

Iulia turned and left without eating. The table was so quiet that Franni could hear Iulia's footfalls down the creaky hallway and the front door slamming as she went out.

"She's right," said Alli. "Maestro Monteverdi should trust us to sing his music."

"Absolutely," said Georgia. "We don't need these fancy singers from Florence."

"Yeah," agreed the others. "That's right."

Franni dared to open her mouth. "I'm sure Maestro just wants it to be as good as possible."

Saying that was a mistake. Every eye turned toward Franni as slits of anger. Every mouth pressed into a frown. "Stay out of it, Franni," snapped Alli. "You don't know what you're talking about."

The girls turned away to talk to each other, and Franni felt alone again.

"Hello? Franni? Are you here?" The voice of Stella, Maria's assistant, floated through the house. "Franni? Come, child!"

"Your nursemaid's calling you," sneered one of the girls, and the others erupted with cruel laughter. As Franni left the dining room, she looked straight at Alli. Her sister lowered her eyes as if she couldn't bear to meet Franni's gaze.

She'd deal with her stuck-up sister later. Franni ran toward the front of the house to see what Stella wanted. Stella was closing the front door with one hand and clutching a piece of paper and two small pouches in the other. "These things are for you," she said.

Puzzled, Franni took them. One pouch was red; it contained twenty florins. The other was black and contained quite a lot more money. On the paper Franni recognized Natalia's scrawl. "48 forest-green braided silk tassels," it read. At the bottom was an address for Signore Samuel Soncino, Cloth Merchant.

Stella waited a moment for Franni to finish reading, then said, "The messenger boy told me you're to go fetch these tassels right away. The twenty florins is for your cab fare." Franni was shocked. She'd never ridden by herself in a cab before. How like a noble lady she would feel! Stella continued, "The black bag is the money for the tassels."

"Why does *she* get to go?" Behind her, Franni found a few curious choristers. "What are the tassels for?"

Stella wrapped a shawl around Franni's shoulders. To the girls, she said, "The tassels will be used on special costumes for the Caccini women."

As the moans of "That's not *fair*!" and "Why don't *we* get tassels?" grew louder, Stella pushed Franni out the door.

"Carriage is waiting," she said. "The driver is named Macchio. He's well trusted, and he'll look after you. Don't dawdle. Natalia needs these tassels quickly."

Franni ran down the front walkway toward the one-horse carriage standing at the curb. The driver opened the coach door and helped her in as he would a duchess. "To Soncino's shop, Signorina?" he asked. When Franni nodded and offered him the address, Macchio held up his hand. "Signora Natalia told me the location. Won't take long to get there."

It was a perfect spring day, so Franni leaned her head out the window and watched the town of Mantua roll by. She even waved to a little kid playing ball in the street and a handsome soldier guarding a very fancy house. *Alli would enjoy this*, Franni found herself thinking before remembering she was mad at her sister.

They passed a stunning marble mansion. "Who lives there?" she called up to Signore Macchio.

"A Medici, Signorina."

Franni recognized the name of the wealthiest family in Italy, if not the whole world. She couldn't help trying to peek inside, to see if she could spy any actual Medicis were having breakfast or reading a book. But they went by too fast for her to get a good look.

Soon they had left the richest part of town. The buildings became a little more cracked and worn out, the streets a little dirtier. Franni noticed that people wore darker, thicker clothes. Many of the men had beards and curls of hair flowing down past their ears. There was a yellow star sewn into the fabric of each man's coat. Franni couldn't stop staring. When she latched gazes with a boy about her age, she lowered her eyes, embarrassed.

"Here's Soncino's shop, Signorina," said Macchio. He climbed down from the driver's seat and opened her door, helping her to the street. "I'll wait right here, miss, and take you straight home."

Franni knew she shouldn't be nervous, but she was anyway. The entrance to the fabric shop was just a few paces away. The people out on the street greeted each other in a friendly way. But something about this place seemed strange to Franni.

"Good morning, miss." The boy she'd seen from the coach stood near her now. He had the curls at his ears and the star on his coat. Once Franni looked at his face, she saw that he also had an easy smile. The boy bowed politely. "My name is David Soncino. Please allow me to welcome you to my father's shop."

Without waiting for her reply, the boy strode forward and opened the shop door. Holding it open, he looked at Franni expectantly. What could she do but go inside?

Although the sun shone brightly that day, the shop was dark and candlelit. A black-haired man with a skullcap and beard leaned over a ledger book.

"Father?" said David, "You have a customer."

The man peered up from his book. Franni was struck by the strong line of his cheekbone and his kind eyes. "Ah, good morning!" said Signore Soncino.

"Good morning, Signore." Franni curtsied and held out her note.

The merchant squinted and angled the paper into the candlelight. "Oh, my. What a large order. One moment, if you please, while I see if I have so many tassels in stock. May I be so bold as to ask, for which household are you collecting them?"

Franni thought about the question and gave what she thought was the right answer. "For Duke Vincenzo Gonzaga's household."

"Oh!" The merchant lost his balance for a moment. "Highest priority then, eh? David, offer our guest a chair!"

"Yes, Father." David moved a pile of embroidered cloth off a chair and motioned for Franni to sit down.

His father's voice could be heard from the back room. "And are these tassels for draperies to cover the Palazzo walls, to keep out the chill? Or perhaps for bed coverings?"

Franni called out. "No, Signore. They're for costumes in Maestro Monteverdi's theatrical show, *Arianna*."

"Ohh! That's wonderful!" Signore Soncino reappeared, clutching an awkward bundle. David rushed to help him with it. The merchant was smiling broadly. "Maestro Monteverdi's music is exquisite. So emotional. Are you allowed to watch rehearsals?"

The three of them had a delightful conversation about *Arianna* and the music of the great Monteverdi. Franni would have been happy to stay there all day, but Macchio came in and reminded her rather gruffly that Natalia was waiting and they needed to leave right away.

"I do hope to have the privilege of seeing you again, Signorina," said David. Franni thought he sounded like a courtier at the Duke's Palazzo.

"I'm Franni," she blurted out. Once she'd said it, her nickname seemed too informal and childish. "Francesca Ategnati." She curtsied clumsily and rushed out with the bundle in her arms.

CHAPTER 12

WITH MACCHIO'S HORSE PULLING double-quick, Franni was in front of Maria's house in no time. She climbed down and gave the driver his twenty florins. He must have been late for another job, since he flicked the reins and clattered away the moment the door opened and Maria stepped out.

Maria did not look pleased to see Franni. "What are you *doing* here? Where's that blasted driver going?"

Helplessly, Franni held out the bundle of tassels. "But I brought these back, like you told me."

"Not *here,* child." Maria shook her head. "What would we need them *here* for? They're needed at the Palazzo, foolish girl."

Franni felt the world spin. She tried to stammer out an apology. "Oh, I'm so, oh, goodness—"

"Never mind." Maria turned Franni around by the shoulders and pointed toward the Duke's residence. "Just go. Hurry. My poor sister's getting another gray hair for every minute you're late."

Franni ran. It was more of a lurch, since she had the bundle pressed tightly against her chest with both arms and therefore couldn't lift her skirts. She tripped a few times and muddied her hems in more puddles than she could count. It was only a few blocks from Maria's house to the Palazzo, but it felt as long as the road from Verona to Mantua.

With the Palazzo so close that Franni could recognize who was on guard duty, she tried to pick up the pace. But, out of nowhere, a man and woman were suddenly standing in front of her. Franni stopped fast, dropping her bundle. Several of the green tassels rolled out onto the damp paving stones.

"Aw, we are so, so, so sorry," said the woman as Franni scrambled breathlessly to retrieve the tassels. "Aren't we sorry, Uncle?" Neither grownup moved to help Franni.

The man spoke up. "She must be headed to the Palazzo with all those pretty baubles, wouldn't you say, Auntie?"

The couple had strange accents, which Franni couldn't quite place. And when she looked up at them, their mischievous eyes gave her a definite creepy feeling. "I have no money with me," she said, assuming they were planning to rob her. "And these tassels are the property of the Duke of Mantua. You'd better not mess with them." She didn't feel as brave as she hoped she sounded.

The woman gave a very fake gasp of astonishment. "Ooh, the Duke of Mantua. Did you hear that, Uncle?"

"Very impressive, Auntie." The man bent over, clearly challenging the seams in his trousers, and plucked up a single tassel that had come to rest near his shoe. "Do you suppose he'll dangle them from his coat?" While the woman screeched out a laugh, the man handed the tassel to Franni, locking her in his gaze. "Auntie and I are looking for our nephew. Perhaps you know him."

Franni relaxed slightly. She didn't like these people, but they hadn't pulled out a knife or threatened her. And surely no one would harm her half a block from the palace guard. "Your nephew? Does he work at the Palazzo?" she asked, trying to sound calm and polite.

"Why, yes," said the woman. Franni noticed that her face was pock-marked. And she seemed uncomfortable in her expensive clothes. Now that she thought about it, the couple's strange accent might be the sound of uneducated people pretending to be above their class. "What's his name, ma'am?"

The woman spread her rough face into a disturbing grin. Franni was fixated on her broken front tooth when she spat out a familiar name. "Luca de Rore."

Franni forced herself not to exclaim. She tried not to let the alarm she felt show on her face. The woman twittered on. “Such a handsome boy, right, Uncle?” The man nodded. He had a faint scar across the back of one hand. “Tall with wavy brown hair.”

“Chestnut brown,” said the man. “And he’s a singer. You seem to be involved with sewing. You make costumes, perhaps? The Duke does like his theatrical entertainments, eh? Perhaps you know our Luca.”

The woman stepped in front of the man. “We only want to go into the Palazzo to see him,” she oozed.

“To surprise our darling nephew,” the man added, “who hasn’t seen his beloved Auntie and Uncle for many a long year.”

“So?” The woman pushed her face inches from Franni’s. “Will you take us into the Palazzo and point out our dear Luca? We haven’t seen him since he was a little boy.”

Franni’s heart pounded. Inside her head, she heard Iulia’s threat. *You’ll pay for this.* As fast as she could form the words, she shouted, “No, sorry, I don’t know him and you’ll have to ask someone else, I’m very late, goodbye.” And she practically flew the final half block to the guard’s checkpoint.

“Hey, there,” said the guard. “Slow down. I’ve got to check your bundle.” This guard, Paulo, was always friendly to Franni. He’d told her once that he had a daughter her age. While Franni held the cloth sack steady in her arms and tried to keep her heart steady as well, Paulo poked through the dozens of tassels. “They squirm like little green puppies,” he joked. Franni tried to smile.

“Are you okay?” Paulo asked, leaning closer to her. “Are you crying?”

For a long moment, Franni considered telling Paulo all about the weird couple she’d just met. But when she glanced down the road behind her, she could see no sign of them. Nor could she think of anything in particular from their conversation that Paulo would find suspicious. So she just shook her head and curtsied. “I’m fine, thank you. I’m just late. Afraid I’ll get in trouble.”

"Well, off you go, then." Paulo's gentle smile nearly made Franni burst into tears. She clasped her bundle close, as if it were her own precious Babbo, and hurried in through the servants' entrance.

There was nobody in the sewing room, so Franni ran down the hall. When she lunged into the rehearsal room, she found it full of people but strangely quiet. Franni sidled through the crowd until she was next to Edgardo.

"Caccini's women," he whispered.

The members of the chorus, the solo singers, instrument players, even crew and seamstresses, all stood looking at a group of people in the center of the room.

Maestro Monteverdi, Signore Rinuccini, and Signore Striggio were exchanging pleasantries with six extraordinary women. Although the women were all different sizes, they shared a calm self-confidence that reminded Franni of her mother. She admired them right away. And, most amazing of all, Maestro Monteverdi's face was relaxed and happy.

"I didn't think he could smile," Franni whispered to Edgardo.

He snickered. But when he looked up into her face, his brow creased with concern. "Did something happen to you?"

The urge to tell Edgardo everything overtook Franni, but she knew she needed to control herself. "I'll tell you later. Let's meet in the prop storage room at lunch." Edgardo nodded and turned his attention back to the Caccini women.

The people around Franni started to applaud, and the beautiful women from Florence curtsied with practiced grace.

"Now that we've welcomed our special guests, let's all get back to work, please," called Signore Striggio.

Edgardo grinned at Franni and patted her hand. "We'll talk soon." She tried to grin back, but when he turned and disappeared amid the taller construction crew, she choked back a sob. Lunch seemed like ten years in the future.

Once she got busy, what remained of the morning flew by. Franni was grateful for that. Natalia didn't even have a chance to scold her for being late. Or maybe she hadn't even noticed, what with all the hubbub over the new singers. The poor chief seamstress was frantically trying to get measurements for the six newcomers. Franni went out of her way to be helpful, running errands, taking notes, and pouring wine for the honored guests.

"Why do they get special costumes, anyway?" Franni asked Donata when she reached over onto her table for a pin cushion. "Aren't they supposed to blend into the chorus?"

Donata gave Franni a knowing look. "It's in their contracts."

"What is?"

"That the audience always know when they're singing."

Franni glanced at each Florentine singer in turn. "Are they really that good? Have you heard them?"

Donata breathed out a sigh and her eyes lost focus, like she was calling up a treasured memory. "Last year, they sang in Maestro's tragedy *Orfeo.* They played spirits of the Underworld. And, Franni, they sounded like God's own angels."

Franni tried to imagine such a sound, but the braying of her own name interrupted her. "Franni! Franni!" It was Natalia, trying to get her attention from across the sewing room. "Bring those pins I asked for, for Heaven's sake."

Franni didn't get another moment's rest until a late lunch break.

Edgardo was pacing up and down the corridor. He looked worried. "Where've you been? I've been waiting in the props room, as you asked. Have to go back to work in a minute."

"Sorry," said Franni. "Natalia wouldn't let me go until now." Franni looked around for eavesdroppers, but everyone seemed busy in their own affairs. "Let's talk in that alcove." She led Edgardo down the hallway some twenty paces. The alcove contained a marble bust of Duke Gonzaga. With mock reverence and funny florid hand gestures, Edgardo bowed to it. "Greetings, Your Absolute and Excellent Serene Spectacularity," he said solemnly.

Franni stepped back in alarm. "Shh! You'll get in terrible trouble."

But Edgardo just shrugged. "It's a piece of stone. And these–" he reached up and tapped the sculpture's oversized right ear, "can't actually hear a thing." The sarcastic look dissolved from his face. "So, my Snailnose, tell me what happened. I'm concerned about you."

Knowing there was no time to waste, Franni told him her worst fear. "I think someone else is after you-know-who."

Edgardo shook his head. "Actually, I don't know who. Tell me."

Astonished that he could have forgotten about the missing Duke already, Franni spoke harshly. "Don't you care about anything? Isn't anything important to you?" Her voice dropped to a low whisper. "I mean Luca, obviously."

Edgardo groaned and slapped his forehead. "What, again? I thought I put an end to that nonsense. The Bergamo soldiers left."

"They weren't soldiers," Franni snapped. "Other people were asking about him."

"Look, Franni," Edgardo said, crossing his arms, "we've done a lot for him already. Maybe we should let his destiny play out. Who are we to get involved, anyway?"

Franni felt a sickening tightness in her stomach. "You promised." She was determined not to make a scene, but she had a strong urge to slap his face. "You promised you'd protect him for my sister's sake." In hopes of making her words cut deeper, she added, "I thought you were my *friend.*"

It was clear from the sadness in his eyes that she'd hurt him. For a moment he seemed to be deciding what to say. "It's not that I don't want to help, Franni. I'm just wondering if we're sticking our noses in where they shouldn't be, you know?"

Franni was ready for that argument. "It's for his freedom."

"What?"

"You said everyone should be allowed to live his own life. So, we're protecting his freedom."

Edgardo smiled slightly. "I did say that, didn't I? It really would serve me well to remember just how smart you are. Okay, tell me all about it."

Now Franni was smiling, too. She described the odd man and woman, and how they claimed to be Luca's "Auntie and Uncle" even though they weren't sure what he looked like. "And it's hard to explain," Franni added, "but it's as if their faces and voices didn't match their clothes. Like they were poorer than they were pretending to be."

"Bounty hunters." Edgardo spat out the words. "Scum of the earth. There's a reward involved, so they show up. They'll do anything, any kind of trickery, to get the money."

Franni was shocked. "Will they hurt him?"

"Well, fortunately, the reward is for the living Duke. Maybe a few scratches or bruises, but that would be the worst of it."

"Still," said Franni, "we should try to keep him from them."

Edgardo nodded grimly. "If we can, we will. Now, I must return to my job, and you should eat something."

He turned to go, but Franni thought of something else she needed to say. "Edgardo, wait." He stopped. "There was another man. Much scarier. He's never spoken to me, but I've seen him twice. He stares, and his face is like a nightmare."

Edgardo's jaw was tense. "Describe the face."

She shivered just picturing it. "He's got leathery skin, and his eyes are uneven against his nose."

Weaving slightly as if he might faint, Edgardo reached out to the wall for balance. "Pietro Fucilli," he breathed.

"Who's that?" Franni felt the hairs rise along her arms. "A bounty hunter?"

Edgardo shook his head. "Much, much more dangerous." Sweat beaded on his forehead. "Very bad news."

Franni was freezing with fear. "He'll harm Luca?" She made herself ask her true question. "Will he kill him?"

At that, Edgardo pulled himself together. He spoke firmly, with a determined look on his face. "I don't know what he wants. I do know that, if he'd wanted to kill that spoiled kid, he'd have done so by now."

"How do you know so much about this Pietro—?"

Edgardo put his finger to his lips before she could say the name *Fucilli.* "Let's just say, I've been mixed up in some things I wouldn't want a nice girl like you to hear."

A little offended, Franni countered, "Maybe I'm not such a nice girl."

But Edgardo laughed. "Oh, believe me, my precious Snailnose. You are a nice girl. And you must never pretend otherwise."

"Ruggiero!" the foreman bellowed. Without another word, Edgardo turned and walked into the rehearsal room. Franni watched him go, thinking about bounty hunters and much scarier men. She didn't feel very hungry for lunch.

CHAPTER 13

WHEN FRANNI DIDN'T SEE THE cockeyed man or the strange couple for the next several days, she began to think she'd imagined all of it. Even if Luca really was the Duke, it certainly seemed like everyone had stopped looking for him. Or, even more likely, the folks in Bergamo had decided they didn't want him after all.

"Who could blame them?" Franni asked herself, watching Luca strut and brag among the women of the chorus. Alli was still crazy about him, and still insisted they would get married.

"So, where's your ring?" Franni asked, just to needle her one day while they were walking home. "If you're getting married, he should've given you a ring."

"Well, *obviously*, he can't give me a ring until he's been made Duke officially."

Franni was enjoying this. "Not even a little ring? A cheap one? To prove how much he loves you?" She made kissing sounds in the air.

Alli's exasperated sign sounded like water thrown over embers. "Why should he bother with that? Soon he'll be able to give me a beautiful ring."

It was just too much fun and Franni couldn't stop. "Oh, really? Then he should step up now and admit he's the Duke. Maestro Monteverdi doesn't need him. There are plenty of men to sing in the chorus. Maestro doesn't even like him. Why doesn't he just announce that he's Duke Luca?"

"It's Duke Marco," Alli corrected impatiently. "And how dare you even ask that! It's a big step in his life, and he's just not quite ready. Why can't you understand? Maybe you're jealous because you don't get to marry a Duke."

Franni snorted. "Maybe I don't believe he's really the Duke." The words shocked Franni even as they came out of her own mouth.

But Alli was clearly more than shocked. She had tears in her eyes. "What a thing to say! You're the worst sister *ever.*" She ran ahead.

* * *

Franni felt guilty about what she'd said, and Alli avoided her as much as possible in the tight quarters. That night Franni had trouble sleeping. A couple of times she thought she heard Alli weeping in the dark. But when Franni said, "Are you okay?" the sound stopped abruptly.

The next morning, Alli's eyes were red. Franni tried to apologize to her, but Alli kept walking away before Franni could say anything.

At the Palazzo that day, there was a lull in the costume making, at least for Franni. The seamstresses with masterful skills, like Natalia and Donata, never slowed down. But the kind of tasks Franni could manage were all under control for the moment.

That's why Franni happened to be in the rehearsal room when all the excitement started. She noticed a page boy come in leading a veiled woman and an aging soldier with his hat low over his eyes. Franni had never seen a military uniform like that before, so she assumed he was from a foreign land, probably a guest of Duke Gonzaga. She could hear the page pointing things out, as if giving a tour to visitors.

"That cloud there, see, your Graces?" the page said, "It can float up and down, carrying a man."

"Well, is that a fact?" said the soldier, with some kind of accent.

Franni smiled, imagining how impressive that cloud must seem to people not used to Italian know-how.

But it was the veiled woman's reaction that caught Franni's attention. The woman didn't react to the cloud at all. She wasn't looking at it. *What could be more interesting than the cloud?* Franni wondered. The woman seemed to be searching the room, trying to spot something or someone. For no good reason, she gave Franni the chills.

Maestro Monteverdi was engrossed in his rehearsal. In a few days, the company would move to the gigantic new theater building. They would have very little time to get used to it before the performance on May 28. The Maestro seemed desperate to work everyone to the bone while they were still in the rehearsal room.

He clapped his hands sharply. "Tenors!" he called. The music stopped. "Tenors, is it too much to ask you to listen while you sing? The harpsichord is playing a repeating bass note just for you." He turned to the harpsichordist. "Martino, would you kindly demonstrate?"

The harpsichordist fingered the same note over and over with his left hand.

"Lovely. Yes. Most grateful, Martino." Monteverdi bared his teeth at the tenors in a very frightening smile. "So, gentlemen, that is the rhythmic pulse to guide your singing. It is also the sense of excitement, like a quickened heartbeat, you should show with your voice." He flipped a page of his score furiously. "Tenors, step forward and try it again, right from that spot."

The members of the chorus shuffled their positions to let some of the men move to the front. Franni looked again at the veiled woman as the harpsichord started playing its heartbeat. The tenors came in with their line: "Fate brings love and takes love away."

Rather than watching the famed composer at work, like a normal visitor would do, the veiled woman's head swung around slowly. She craned her neck and even rose up on tiptoe.

Monteverdi cut off the singing with a violent arm gesture. "No!" he bellowed. "One of you is late, dragging the beat. You, Luca de Rore! Sing it by yourself!"

Just as Luca stepped forward, the veiled woman turned her head to stare at him. She raised her veil and pointed, shouting. "There he is!"

Franni now recognized "Auntie" and "Uncle" from a few nights before. As the aging soldier drew his sword, Franni screamed, "Edgardo! It's the bounty hunters!"

The chaos that followed lasted only a few seconds, but to Franni it felt like time had stopped. She heard the confused roar around her, but saw everything clearly, like a series of paintings.

The old soldier pulled off his hat, and his gray hair came off with it. There stood the man who had claimed to be Luca's uncle. He took several powerful leaps toward the tenors.

Luca put his hands to his face, and his eyes were wide with fear. The other singers scattered in all directions. Musicians held their instruments above their heads and made for the exits. Striggio and Rinuccini pulled a stunned Monteverdi to safety.

Luca tried to escape, too, but the woman cut him off. Franni could hear Alli cry out, "Leave him alone!" But Luca was trapped. As the woman reached out to grab Luca's right arm from the front, her husband grabbed his left arm from behind.

In a huge voice, the man announced, "We claim bounty on Marco Coriglio D'Espelina, the Second, herediary Duke of Bergamo."

For a few seconds, everyone stopped their frantic motions and turned to stare. The only sounds were dozens of gasps and whispers of "I can't believe it." Alli had Iulia by the collar of her dress, and pointed accusingly at the couple. Iulia started crying and nodded her head. "I had my papa tell them about Luca," she moaned. "I was so mad at you. Oh, Alli, I'm so sorry!"

The man pushed Luca roughly toward the door, but as they stepped forward, Franni heard a familiar voice from above her.

"Unhand him, knave!" Edgardo shouted as he swung down the scaffolding. He landed in front of the fake soldier. "On your guard."

Franni knew that "On your guard" was what people said before a sword fight. But Edgardo had no sword. The bounty hunter drew a long silver blade from his belt. Franni prayed Edgardo wasn't fool enough to challenge a well-armed man with only a bread knife.

"Franni!" Edgardo shouted, pointing beyond her. "My weapon!" She followed his finger to the corner of the room. All she saw was the stage set representing the ocean, which looked like rolling waves when crews turned its crank. "Behind the waves," Edgardo said. "Toss me a sword."

Franni found a pile of swords all right, but they were just wooden props. There wasn't time to argue about it. As Edgardo ran toward Luca, Franni hurled a stage sword at him with both hands. He caught it deftly by its hilt. "I challenge your right to take this man for bounty." Edgardo pointed the thick wooden blade upward at the fake soldier's chest.

His wife burst out laughing. "This must be the court jester," she cackled. To Luca she said, "Come on, Highness. Let's trade you for some gold. I need a new pair of shoes and a holiday in Spain." She yanked at Luca's elbow, but her husband dropped Luca's left arm and stepped toward Edgardo.

"Just ignore the half-man," she said crossly, "and let's get out of here."

Edgardo took a swaggering step forward and tapped the end of his sword against the man's coat. "You afraid to fight me, a big man like you?"

The man made a strange growling sound and raised his real, steel sword in an arc toward Edgardo. Edgardo blocked skillfully with his wooden sword, but the metal sliced right through his blade. "Another one, Franni!"

Franni tossed wooden swords to Edgardo one after the other as he shattered them.

"Run, Luca!" Alli screamed. He did.

Franni was too busy to see what he where he went, but a moment later she heard the clanking of armor and a gruff male voice yell, "Halt, in the name of his Serene Highness, Duke of Mantua!"

Everyone froze. Franni turned to see two large armored guards just inside the entrance to the rehearsal room. One had the bounty-hunting woman by the hair. The other had Luca by the back of the neck.

"Let him go!"

Franni was amazed when Alli and Iulia rush together and began pummeling Luca's captor. Bare fists rang against metal armor, but the guards paid no attention to the furious girls. Franni noticed a motion out of the corner of her eye. It was the man bounty hunter, trying to sneak out. But Franni still had a wooden sword in her hands, and she moved faster than he did. With the sword outstretched, she lunged toward his feet. He pitched headfirst, right into the arms of a third guard who'd just entered.

"Many thanks, Signorina," the guard said, nodding at Franni.

A fussy man with a gray beard had come in next to the third guard. He spoke directly to the snarling woman. "You are Mirella and Lorenzo Perez."

"Yeah? What's it to you?" She spat on the floor near the gentleman's blue velvet robe.

He shook his head and breathed deeply, as if calming himself at the sigh of something very unpleasant. "I am Giovanni Enzio, banker for his Highness, Duke Gonzaga. The reward for delivering the Duke of Bergamo shall be claimed by the coffers of Mantua."

"That's robbery!" the woman cried.

"It sure is," agreed her accomplice. "We found him. We should get the money."

"But that," said Signore Enzio, "is not in the best interest of the city of Mantua." The old banker sighed and scratched his beard. "Of course, there will only be a reward *if*—" He paused and looked at his rapt audience. "*If* this is truly the heir to the dukedom of Bergamo."

Alli and Iulia tripped over each other's exclamations of "Look at his tall build!" and "He has the wavy brown hair!" and "Check his birthmark!"

Everyone in the room started chanting, "Check his birthmark, check his birthmark." Franni and the rest of the company stepped in closer, forming a circle around the guards, the bounty hunters, Signore Enzio, and Luca. "Check his birthmark," Franni said with this others, noticing how sick and ashen Luca's face was. *He must really be afraid to be the Duke*, she thought.

As one guard turned Luca around and held his arms, the banker pulled up Luca's tunic to reveal his lower back.

"No!" wailed Alli.

"Oh!" gasped Mirella and Lorenzo Perez.

"Ha!" cried the banker.

Franni blinked her eyes a few times to be sure she could trust them. There was a brown mark on Luca's back, but it was definitely not shaped like a fish. It was more like a giant smudge. The banker tore the lace collar from Mirella's dress and daubed his sweaty forehead with it. Then he rubbed the damp rag across Luca's back. The "birthmark" disappeared completely.

"Faker!" screamed Alli.

"Horrible monster!" cried Iulia.

The two girls hugged each other, sobbing.

No more dreams of marrying a duke, thought Franni, and she actually felt sorry for her sister.

"Luca de Rore," announced one of the guards, "you are hereby arrested for impersonating someone of noble lineage." He marched Luca roughly out the door.

"You two," said another guard to the bounty hunters. "You'll be fined the amount of the reward, for disturbing the peace and security of the Duke's Palazzo."

"We can't afford that!" said the woman.

Her husband agreed, "That's an outrage."

The guard smiled smugly. "Either that, or hard labor. You choose." Signore and Signora Perez quieted down and followed the banker meekly from the room.

Singers, instrument players, and crew members buzzed around the edges of the room, whispering excitedly. Maestro Monteverdi came back into the center and looked around nervously. Signore Striggio, always the calm one, put his hand on the Maestro's shoulder. "To your places, please," Striggio called. "There's work to be done."

Alli and Iulia were still comforting each other, so Franni searched for Edgardo to talk to. She found him sitting in the corner behind the mechanical waves. Franni ducked under the giant blue and white corkscrew and pushed the last two remaining wooden swords to the side.

"Wasn't that amazing?" she laughed. "I *knew* Luca wasn't really the Duke, but I couldn't quite put my finger on why." She rearranged her skirts and sat on the floor next to Edgardo. "Poor Alli, though. This is very hard on her. Maybe we could do something nice for her just to cheer her up. You could make her some bread! Would you mind doing that, Edgardo?"

He didn't answer. She leaned closer to him. "Edgardo?

She saw blood on his shirt.

CHAPTER 14

"EDGARDO? ARE YOU HURT?" Franni leaned close to his face, touching Edgardo's cheek with her fingers. His eyes sprang open, making her jump back.

"I'm good as gold, Snailnose. Is this even my blood?" Edgardo tried to get up, but winced and slumped back down. "Okay, I guess it's my blood."

"I'll fetch the doctor," said Franni.

"No!" Edgardo grabbed the blue corkscrew of the wave prop and pulled himself up to his feet. "Don't be ridiculous. I don't need a doctor. See?" He wobbled, and Franni steadied him. "See, I'm fine."

"At least let me help dress your wound," begged Franni. "My mama taught me how."

But Edgardo pulled away from her and staggered toward the exit. He left smudged red fingerprints on the wall as he grabbed it with every few steps. Franni noticed that no one else offered to help him. Even Alli backed away as he passed. *It's up to me,* she thought with a sigh, *whether he wants help or not.*

She followed after him, watching him limp down the hallway. Having a pretty good idea where he was heading, Franni took a moment to grab some scraps of cloth from the sewing room. They might come in handy for covering his wound. When she stepped back into the hallway, she could see Edgardo slip into the props storage room, just as she'd expected.

A few other people passed her in the corridor. There was a maid with a bundle of bed clothes, a guard making his rounds, a violinist muttering to himself about a broken string, and a priest. Franni considered asking the priest to come in and see her injured friend, but she was afraid Edgardo would be rude to him. That might anger the Almighty just when they needed his help. So she let the priest go by without a word.

Franni opened the door of the props room without knocking. It was very dark except for a single torch at the back of the room. Moving carefully so she wouldn't rip on any wooden beams or paint buckets, Franni picked her way toward the light. She had another reason to go slowly. She was afraid of what she might find. Was Edgardo dying? Her pulse raced and her feet resisted stepping forward.

She could hear Edgardo scuffling and panting behind an old wooden backdrop painted as a clump of trees. Steeling her nerves, Franni pasted a smile on her face and prepared to greet Edgardo calmly.

But just then Edgardo stepped out from behind the trees, his bloody shirt crumpled in his hands. "Aaah!" they both shouted at once.

Franni found words first. "Sorry, I just wondered how you were doing." She bent and squinted at his wound. "Oh, that cut doesn't look so bad. Here, daub it with this cloth."

Edgardo didn't take the cloth. Instead, he looked at Franni as if she were a ghost who'd risen from the dead right before his eyes. "Out," he whispered through his clenched jaw. He held up his bloody shirt, and Franni thought he might throw it at her. But instead he backed away toward the wooden trees, growling, "How dare you come in here, you stupid little child? Get out." Edgardo disappeared behind the set.

Franni felt cold and dizzy. She pressed the cloth scraps to her stomach, imagining her doll, Babbo. But she was determined not to cry in front of this horrid man, who wasn't anything at all like her dear friend Edgardo. Still, the tears were coming. Franni lifted her skirts and sprang gingerly over all the obstacles in her path to the door. She tripped a few times, but stopped herself from yelping. She knew if she made any sound, she'd start to sob and wouldn't be able to stop.

Once she'd reached the hallway, she bit her lip and sprinted to the sewing room. It was lunchtime, so the other seamstresses were too busy chatting to pay attention to Franni. In that safe haven, she buried her face in the cloth and cried. She curled up in a corner with her arms and head on her knees, thinking about home. Her real home, Verona. Her parents' house, which had also been her grandparents' house. Two stories, with pretty green furniture. Green was Mama's favorite color.

She pictured Papa's office, where he'd run his shipping business. Franni remembered sitting on his knee when she was very young, and waving at the customers. Those businessmen would all be serious at first, pretending not to notice Franni as they placed orders and discussed contracts with Papa. But, by the time they left, most of them would be smiling back at her.

"Franni," Papa used to say, "you're better for business than ads posted all over town." And Mama would shake her head and say, "Just you be careful, Luigi Ategnati. Before you know it, she'll be so smart, she'll be running your business for you."

In spite of her misery, Franni smiled when those words echoed in her memory. She couldn't help wondering what Mama and Papa must think, looking down on her now. She was sewing beautiful costumes, which would please Mama. She was working for a wealthy patron. Papa would approve of that. And, of course, they would burst their seams with pride over Alli, singing for the great Maestro Monteverdi.

Suddenly Franni longed to talk to Alli, the only person alive who really knew her and understood what she'd been through. Franni wiped her face and straightened her hair before heading out to search for her sister.

Because it was less than a week until the performance, the Maestro often made his singers and orchestra work during lunch. Therefore, Franni was not surprised to hear music as she entered the rehearsal room. But it was not the music she expected to hear.

One of Caccini's women from Florence was singing to an absolutely silent crowd. "That doesn't sound like it's from *Arianna*," Franni said aloud.

"Shh!" hissed a bass singer leaning against the wall. "That's a song by Giulio Caccini. He wrote it for his daughter, Francesca, to sing."

Excited that the great Maestro Caccini had named his daughter Francesca, Franni listened closely. The harpsichord and the lute player plucked chords. A man held his viola da gamba between his knees, pulling his bow across the strings in a slow, mournful bass line. And then the singer came in.

The woman's voice was shimmering gold and silk. It was softest ermine fur and darkest heartbreak. "Beautiful Amarillys," she sang, "Don't you believe that you're my heart's desire?" The music snaked around the painful words, choking the life out of a sad lover's hope.

During the song, Franni barely breathed or blinked. When it was done, no one applauded, but many people were weeping.

Alli and Iulia stepped forward to congratulate the singer and hug her. Franni, curious to overhear, pushed closer through the musicians milling around.

"That was such a beautiful song," sighed Iulia.

"Isn't it wonderful?" said the singer. "It's quite famous. Have you never sung it?"

When Iulia and Alli glanced at each other, the singer seemed embarrassed. "Oh, I meant no disrespect. You're so busy with the brilliant Maestro Monteverdi, why should you bother to learn anyone else's songs?"

Monteverdi, standing nearby, bowed stiffly at the compliment. The Florentine singer took the Mantuan singers by the hand. "Still, you must allow me to give you the sheet music as a gift." Alli and Iulia beamed with pleasure.

Everything was friendly again between those two girls, it seemed. And once again, Franni was left out of the circle. She was starting to feel sorry for herself when Alli caught her eye and gave her a surprisingly warm smile. "Iulia," she said, "you and the ladies go on to lunch. I'll be along shortly."

Franni was delighted to see Alli step toward her leaving her friends behind.

"Hi," said Franni.

"Hi," Alli replied. She looked at the floor, then back up at Franni. "Is your friend okay?"

Franni just shrugged. Edgardo was the last person she wanted to talk about. "Are *you* okay?" she asked Alli. "You know, after what happened with Luca?"

Alli straightened her skirts and shook her head. "He let us all think he was the Duke. Didn't he know we'd figure out he was lying?"

For some reason, Franni felt a glimmer of sympathy for the fake Duke. "Maybe he just wanted some attention." She laughed. "I guess you won't be marrying a duke after all."

She'd said it kindly, but Alli's eyebrows shot up. "What do you mean?"

"Well, Luca's not the Duke."

"That's right," said Alli, as if she'd won an argument.

Franni was confused. "Well, now you don't have a duke to marry."

Alli's lips curled into an impish smile. "*Yet.* The Duke of Bergamo must be around here somewhere."

"*What*?" Franni coughed. "You still think he's hiding in Mantua?" She stomped her foot in protest. "Honestly, I don't think there's a Duke at all."

"Of course there's a Duke." Alli's soprano laughter pealed like a happy love song. "There *has* to be. He must be somewhere."

Franni smiled. "You're hopeless, Alessandra Ategnati. And just you wait. I bet you'll fall in love with a cobbler or a cook instead of some fellow with a fancy palace."

Leaning toward her sister, Alli whispered, "Just between you and me, I'd settle for an admiral in the navy."

"Wouldn't he be gone to sea most of the time?" asked Franni.

"Maybe that would make him the perfect husband!" The sisters giggled until they were bent double.

They started down the corridor to see if there was any more food left for lunch. But before they got that far, they heard a few little squeals of panic. It sounded like somebody had seen a mouse. And it was coming from the sewing room.

The idea of a mouse wasn't very surprising. Mantua was a city, after all, and rats and mice liked to live where people were crowded together. The surprising thing was what followed all the squealing.

"Franni? Franni?" came the voice from the sewing room. "Where is that girl?"

Hearing Natalia call her name, Franni ran forward. "I'm right here," she called as she grabbed the door jamb and swung into the room. "What's going on?"

Donata held a large glass bowl in her hands. Her lips were pulled back in disgust. Natalia pointed at the bowl. "Somebody left this for you." She handed Franni a small rectangle of fine linen paper. Three words were written across it in elegant penmanship:

FOR FRANCESCA ATEGNATI

"That's me," said Franni. "Who left it?"

Donata shrugged. "Must've been while I was eating."

"Or napping at your work," said Natalia, looking sharply at the older woman.

"So, what did I get?" Franni took the bowl carefully in both hands. In it, a perfect pink rose lay on its side. "Oh, how pretty!"

Alli stepped forward and took a peek. "Uh-oh. I think little Franni has a sweetheart."

Franni felt herself blush. "I do *not.*"

Donata pushed her gnarly old finger into the bowl. "I *hope* this isn't from your sweetheart. Look what's on the stem."

Franni leaned into the bowl. There was something gray and round on the rose stem. It was definitely not a leaf or a thorn.

"Disgusting!" Alli exclaimed. "It's a snail."

"If that's from a secret admirer," said Natalia, "he certainly has disturbing taste in pets."

"It's creepy," agreed Donata.

But Franni didn't think it was creepy. She held the rose to her round, snail-shaped nose, and silently accepted Edgardo's apology.

CHAPTER 15

"CAN YOU BELIEVE IT'S ONLY two days until we perform this thing?" Edgardo held out a sack of treacled walnuts to Franni. They were looking at a huge, unfinished wooden building on the Via San Giorgio.

Franni popped a nut into her mouth and crunched down on it. The burst of spice sweetness made her eyes water. "How will they ever finish this theater on time?" Men were crawling everywhere on the structure, pounding nails, measuring, sawing and sanding. "Natalia says it's supposed to hold four thousand people in the audience."

"I heard six thousand." Edgardo laughed and bit into a walnut. "Six thousand of his Highness's closest friends. And they say he's had to tell his own loyal knights in Mantua that he won't have room for them."

"Really? Then who's coming?"

As they talked, they strolled toward the back entrance of the new building. Edgardo said, "Well, the Duke's nephew is marrying Princess Margarite of Savoy."

"Where's Savoy? That's a funny name for a town."

"France."

Franni always found these international royal marriages very confusing. "Her family's coming from France for the wedding?"

"Yes, and all sorts of other people the Duke needs to show respect to. Six thousand of them, apparently. He doesn't want to offend anyone important."

They showed their papers to a guard, who waved them in through a bare wooden door. Franni sneezed from the smell of sawdust and paint. "Why would His Highness need to impress all those thousands of people? Isn't being the Duke enough?"

Edgardo sneezed twice. "How much do you think this wedding will cost? The Duke has commissioned Maestro Monteverdi's opera, some plays, some concerts, plus he has to pay for food and lodging for all the guests for a week." One more sneeze. "Aaa-*choo*! They always come in threes." Edgardo wiped his nose on his sleeve. "Anyway, I heard it's costing more than the last wedding in the Medici family."

Franni stopped in the middle of the narrow passageway. "But the Medicis are the richest family anywhere."

Edgardo kept on walking. "That's what I've heard. And the Duke is really not so rich, although he spends like a Medici. The city of Mantua has to borrow money for all this wedding fuss. Not to mention all the other expensive art and theater the Duke commissions." Stepping closer to Franni, he whispered, "I hear His Highness also likes games of chance."

Franni was too shocked to speak at the thought of Mantua's leader gambling like a common ruffian. She just shook her head and wondered about all the gorgeous buildings and sculptures and paintings in Mantua she'd been taking for granted.

She and Edgardo had been wandering through the corridors for a while and Franni was about to say they were lost. But a man's voice called, "Hey, it's Ruggiero!" Franni recognized the foreman from the *Arianna* construction crew. He motioned for them to follow. "This way to the stage."

They tromped through a labyrinth of dark hallways. Around each corner, more and more men were working. When they finally reached the stage, the view from the wings reminded Franni of a seaport. There must have been a hundred men, painting, shifting backdrops, screwing boards together. And up above, like sailors clambering up to a the crow's nest on a ship, more men worked. A gigantic cloth–one Franni had helped measure–billowed for a moment as the crew draped it over a prop throne for King Theseus.

Franni couldn't stop herself from saying, "I do hope these sailors have a safe voyage to Africa."

Most of the men nearby glanced Franni's way with a puzzled look. But Edgardo got the joke. Pulling a long silk handkerchief from his jacket, he waved it around and pranced onto the stage. "Oh, do come back safe and sound to your loving wifey!" he called upward in a high-pitched falsetto. Franni giggled as he pressed the back of his hand to his forehead. "Ah, woe is me. 'Tis a long, perilous trip across the wide Mediterranean Sea."

One of the construction workers called down from the scaffolding, "We'll be fine, so long as we avoid sea monsters that look like *you*."

Another voice called out through the laughter. "Don't worry. That one's too tiny to harm the likes of us." That won a good round of guffaws from all the men. Even Edgardo chuckled.

Franni watched a group of workers on the scaffolding. "Are they setting up the cloud mechanism?"

"They are," said Edgardo. "If it's built right, it should move in the same way it did in the rehearsal room. If you'll excuse me, I should join their work." He added in a loud, theatrical voice, "Heaven knows, I can see they're doing it wrong without my help."

A burly man, who looked too heavy to be balancing up so high, shouted down, "We can manage just fine without the likes of you, Ruggiero."

Edgardo snorted. "Oh, please. That cloud is more likely to drizzle rain of gold than to move up and down, considering how these clowns are putting it together."

The laughing and hooting all around her reminded Franni again of a rough, portside scene. And she knew she didn't belong there. "I should report back to Natalia," she said. "She wants me to let her know what to expect at the new theater."

When she curtsied slightly to say goodbye to Edgardo, a few men installing the wave crank cackled. “Ooh, everyone bow before the great Lord Half-Man,” one of them said.

Edgardo grinned, but Franni felt bad for him. *What a brave front he puts on,* she thought. *He must endure teasing every single day.* Favoring her friend with one more smile, she hurried into the corridors behind the stage. She became confused only twice, and within minutes was back outside. Now it was the afternoon sun that made her sneeze.

It was a perfect spring day. A light breeze carried the scent of flowering trees. Franni looked longingly at the gardens next to the Castle of St. George, near the new theater. She was in no hurry to return to the stuffy Palazzo. What could be the harm in spending a few minutes in the gardens? Natalia was waiting for her, of course, but Franni could tell her she’d been delayed at the theater.

As she crossed over to the garden pathway, Franni tried to think of a believable reason for being late. But the rainbow of colors around her were too distracting. “Lies are never worth it, anyway,” she advised a fat bumble bee lowering itself into a tulip. Franni recognized the rare blossoms from the court gardens in Verona.

A few well-to-do couples strolled arm in arm along the garden paths. Franni envied their freedom. It didn’t seem to her that wealthy people ever had to be anywhere or do anything. *It must be nice,* she thought. *If I were the Duke of Bergamo, I’d come out of hiding and do nothing but stroll around lovely gardens all day long.*

She pictured poor, foolish Luca being dragged from the rehearsal room and shook her head. But she was as embarrassed for herself as for him. She’d fallen for his act just like Alli had. “The only difference is,” she explained to a red-winged blackbird pecking at a spider, “I wasn’t in love with him.”

The gleam of yellow blossoms caught Franni’s eye. She turned onto another path to have a closer look. Passing under a trellis entwined with bluebells, Franni found herself in a whole new section of the gardens. A golden sea of daffodils surrounded a fountain. In the middle of the marble pool, a marble boy poured water from a marble urn. The urn was never emptied, and the sound of its endless trickling comforted Franni like a lullaby.

Facing the fountain, in the shade of a row of linden trees, Franni saw a woman resting on a bench. She had a whole brood of children with her, from a boy about Franni's age down to a little tot just figuring out how to walk. The children all wore expensive clothing of fine material embroidered with designs and decorated with lace. But the woman had on a plain dress of gray wool. She was neat and clean, but Franni could tell that she wasn't wealthy. She had a pleasant smile, so Franni went over to say hello.

"Are you their governess?" Franni asked. She was suddenly very lonely for her own governess, Signora Stassi, back in Verona.

"That's right, child," said the woman on the bench. She had a much sweeter manner than Signora Stassi. "I'm Signorina Angelica. Won't you sit with us awhile?"

"Oh, that's very kind of you," said Franni, "but I really must be getting—"

"We have currant biscuits," interrupted Angelica, holding up a bulging cloth sack. "Plenty to share. Please, at least, take one with you."

"I want a biscuit!" shouted the toddler, stretching out his hands toward the bag.

Angelica nodded and opened the bag. Within seconds, all six children had gathered right up against her skirts. She smiled at Franni, showing a dimple in each cheek. "It's story time, if you'd care to join us."

Franni was under a spell, transported back to a simpler, happier time with her family. Forgetting about Mantua and Natalia and *Arianna*, she took a seat on the grass at Angelica's feet. A girl of about seven handed Franni a biscuit. "You're pretty," the girl said. "May I sit by you?"

Franni nodded. She stroked the girl's black hair with one hand and ate her biscuit with the other.

"Marcello?" said the governess to the eldest boy. "Bring me that acorn near your foot."

The boy did so, grinning shyly at Franni as he reached past her. Franni grinned back, looking at him just long enough to admire his deep brown eyes. Then she looked down at her hands, feeling the blush in her cheeks.

Angelica took the acorn and held it up between thumb and forefinger. "What do you see, children?"

"An acorn!" they all cried, including Franni. She wanted very much to be a part of this family, even for a moment. She hadn't truly felt like a child since her mother died.

"So, you all see an acorn?" Angelica raised her eyebrows. "Does no one see anything else?"

"Something to throw at people and squirrels," suggested a boy of about ten. His sister closest to him slapped him on the head. "Cut it out, Cristina," he complained.

"Well, you shouldn't hurt innocent squirrels with acorns," she said.

Angelica clapped her hands twice. "I don't recall asking what uses we have for acorns." Her eyes were shining with excitement, and Franni thought she must be the best governess ever.

The eldest boy, Marcello, spoke up in a haughty, bored voice. "It's an acorn. How can you pretend it's anything else?"

"I assure you, dear boy, I'm not pretending." Angelica looked at Franni. "And how about our guest? What's your name?"

Franni swallowed hard, suddenly embarrassed. "Francesca." Using her full name was a tribute to Signora Stassi. The old governess never approved of nicknames.

"Well, then, Francesca, what is this?" She held out the acorn. Franni took it in her left palm. Its smooth, hard shell was cool against her skin. She stared hard at it, but it didn't reveal any secrets. "I'm sorry, Signorina," she said quietly. "I just see an acorn." Franni braced herself to be made fun of, but Angelica only smiled more warmly.

"Francesca, you must never apologize because you have something more to learn. There is no offense or shame in that. The offense comes when you have a chance to learn, but you choose not to. Do you understand?"

Franni wasn't sure she did, but still she replied, "Yes, Signora."

Rearranging her skirts a bit and taking the youngest child onto her lap, Angelica said, "And now I shall tell you a story about why we must not simply see an acorn when we look at an acorn."

The children sat up eagerly. Franni couldn't wait for the story. The governess began:

Once upon a time, there was a very rich, very foolish man. One day, he met a woman with great wisdom. Or so she claimed. "You're no wiser than I," he said rudely.

The old woman knew a fool when she saw one. She picked up an acorn from the ground and concealed it in her fist. She thrust her fist against the man's belly. "I'll make you a wager," she said. "I'll bet you your biggest house that what I hold here has greater power than you shall ever know."

"Ha!" said the rich man. "I am as rich as a Medici. No tiny thing that fits in a woman's hand could ever be more powerful than I. But what do you offer as your end of the bargain when I win this wager?"

"My freedom," said the wise woman. "If what I hold is not stronger than you, then I shall become your servant, without pay, until I die."

The rich man always wanted more servants, so he agreed to the bargain readily. "Open your fist," he ordered. The woman did so, revealing the acorn. "Ha! It's just a little acorn." The man did a gleeful dance. "I win! You're my servant now. Go fetch my horse."

But the wise woman simply smiled. "Not so fast. I didn't say it would be stronger than you *now*." With her walking stick, she dug a hold in the soil an dropped the acorn in. "Meet me here in twenty years, and we shall see which of you is more powerful." She turned and hobbled down the road.

Twenty long years passed. The man often thought of the oak tree he knew must be growing all that time. It made him a much less foolish man. He had learned to see what a thing might become, not just how it appeared at the moment. This knowledge allowed him to become richer, find happiness in his life, and bring comfort to others.

Twenty years to the day after his wager with the woman, the man returned to that same place. Of course, a healthy oak tree now grew there, its wide green leaves dappling the sunlight.

After a long wait, the man saw the woman hobbling toward him. She was very, very old. He hurried forward to help her. "Greetings, Auntie," he said kindly. "You've won the bet. I'm prepared to give you the deed to my biggest house."

But the woman shook her white head. "Not at all, sir. I've lost the bet, I'm very pleased to say. Look what you have made of yourself because I showed you the potential of the acorn when you were young. You learned as you grew, and became a better person. There is no greater power than that. You are more powerful than this oak tree, which only grew without learning."

The man was touched by her wisdom, and forgave her debt of servitude. She became his chief counsel for the rest of her days.

Signorina Angelica smiled at the children. Franni sat silent, letting the wonder of the tale and the fragrance of the garden wrap around her. "What a lovely story," said the girl next to her. "We should do it as a play. Act it out. I want to be the wise woman."

At the mention of theater, Franni snapped out of her trance and scrambled to her feet. "Oh, my goodness, I must go! Thank you very much, everyone. I'm so glad I met you!"

Without waiting for their goodbyes, Franni turned and ran out of the magical garden, trying not to picture the look she would surely see on Natalia's face.

CHAPTER 16

"WHERE HAVE YOU BEEN?" Natalia insisted with a severe frown. Franni felt awful, but she couldn't get the words out to explain. "Where on earth have you *been*?" Natalia asked again. But before Franni could answer, she went on, gesturing around the sewing room, "Did you think those dresses would hem themselves? How about those buckles over there? Did you imagine they would attach themselves to those britches out of kindness?"

Franni opened her mouth, but Natalia shushed her with a raised finger. "The new theater is ten minutes from here. All I asked you to do was have a look and take some notes. Yet, you've been gone for hours. And the performance only two days away! Oh, I can't help but notice something else, child." Natalia took Franni by the shoulders and squared her off. "You have crumbs down the front of your dress. So, I ask you again, where have you *been*?"

Trembling, Franni thought frantically for a lie she could tell. Maybe there was a coach accident blocking the streets? Maybe she got lost? Maybe the set crew needed her help with something at the theater? But what about the details of her fib? How would she make Natalia believe her? What if she forgot the details later?

This, she thought, *is why I'm just no good at lying.*

Realizing that calmed her down. With a steady voice, and looking Natalia straight in the eye, she said, "I walked among the flowers at the St. George's Castle gardens, and a storyteller gave me some biscuits." Both for telling the truth and for having such a splendid afternoon, Franni couldn't help being slightly pleased with herself.

Natalia was not amused. "You think this is funny? Do you realize how much trouble you're—"

"The Duke is here!" A voice from the corridor interrupted Natalia's judgment. A page poked his head into the sewing room. "His Most Serene Highness commands your attendance in the rehearsal room. Quick, quick now, ladies."

Sparing two seconds to glare at Franni, Natalia began herding her seamstresses together like a sheepdog. "Come on, now. You heard the boy. Quick, quick. Mustn't keep His Highness waiting."

Franni, relieved to have her punishment delayed, marched down the hall silently with the herd of seamstresses, makeup artists and wig makers, and other *Arianna* crew members. A guard from the Duke's personal retinue opened the rehearsal room doors with a flourish. Inside, all the singers and dancers were gathered in a semicircle. As Franni joined their ranks, she noticed Alli across the room next to Iulia. Alli made a small waving motion and Franni returned the hello.

The center of attention was a group of very important people. Duke Gonzaga sat in a large chair that someone must have dragged in just for him. Maestro Monteverdi stood at his left. Rinuccini and Striggio stood behind the Duke. In a smaller chair, to the Duke's right, sat a woman Franni recognized.

"Is that Madame Andreini, who plays the role of Arianna?" she whispered to Giuseppe, who stood next to her clutching his violin.

"Yes," he whispered back. "Now, hush."

But Franni couldn't resist asking one more question. "They look so serious. Did somebody die?"

"Sshh!" hissed everyone around her.

Duke Gonzaga sat up a bit straighter and cleared his throat. "Company, I have wondrous news." Franni decided that meant nobody had died. "Last night in our apartments, her Highness the Duchess and I were treated to a rare experience." Duke Gonzaga held out his right hand toward Madame Andreini, who looked down and blushed. "This extraordinary actress here previewed for us the lament from the musical tragedy *Arianna*. It was specially written for her by my faithful servants Maestro Monteverdi and Signore Rinuccini."

The men bowed to their patron, who continued. "I do declare, the lament of the lady Arianna is one of the most exquisite songs ever written in the Italian tongue. Its lyrics are so bittersweet and heartwrenching, and Madame Andreini's singing so moving, well—" The Duke took a long, deep sigh. "I do confess the Duchess and I wept when we heard it."

Taking the chair's armrests in each hand, the Duke pushed himself to his feet. "I congratulate you, and predict this musical tragedy will be lauded as the finest such entertainment anyone in Italy and Savoy has ever seen. God bless the tale of *Arianna*. Guards!"

Without another word, his Highness left the room. Franni expected Maestro Monteverdi to swoon with pleasure at the royal compliments. Instead, he was seething.

"Nothing about the music," he muttered. "It's my music that brings those words to life. It's my new style of harmony that makes the heart ache and fills the eyes with tears. My music is the devoted servant of the noble words, and, like all nobles, the words are helpless without their servant."

The Maestro paused in his rant and scanned the crowd accusingly. No one dared to breathe. "What are you gawping at?" he roared. "We have work to do!"

One pleasant result of the Duke's whirlwind visit was how it tempered Natalia's mood. Rather than fire Franni for her lateness, she just gave her extra tasks. But Franni didn't mind. It made the rest of the day go quickly. True, she was exhausted at quitting time, but she was grateful to have a job.

Alli was waiting for her at the servants' exit.

She was alone, which surprised Franni. "No Iulia?'

Alli shrugged. "She has a date with one of the baritone singers."

"She doesn't think he's a duke, does she?" Franni snickered. Alli only smiled slightly, as if she had something else on her mind. They set out along the street in silence.

They were just heading past the toy shop Franni so admired when Alli said, "I heard you saw the new theater. Let's go past it now! You can describe what it's like inside. I must know what to expect when we sing there next week."

It was a short walk out of their way. Franni's stomach growled, and she worried about missing supper at Maria's house, but she was glad to have some time alone with Alli. As they passed the Castle of St. George, the scent of flowers from the gardens was like incense from an exotic land. Franni stopped to sniff the air. She was ready to tell Alli about the governess and the story of the acorn.

But Alli pulled at her arm and pointed to the new theater. "Oh, there it is. My, it's *huge.*" Franni stumbled behind as Alli dragged her toward the wooden building. "All the princes and dukes will be gathered there to hear us. Everyone who's anyone will vie for seats." Alli turned excitedly to Franni. "It holds four thousand people."

Franni grinned, enjoying the rare advantage of knowing more about something than her sister did. "Actually, six thousand."

"Oh!"

"It has two balconies, and the orchestra will sit behind the stage. There are six dressing rooms. And they've already put in the mechanisms to move the cloud and the waves." Franni stopped her report, noticing her sister's face. The moonlight and torchlamps lining the streets lit Alli in a way that made her look just like their mother. It made Franni feel safe and contented. "Mama and Papa would be so proud of you," she admitted to her sister.

Alli turned and smiled. "See? Mantua isn't so bad."

"I don't care what city I'm in right now, so long as I can get some supper," Franni joked, starting down the street. "Let's go home."

As they walked a horse-drawn cart pulled up next to them. Alli kept walking, but Franni looked at it. She was surprised to recognize the driver. "Carlo!" It was the man who'd first given them a ride into the city.

Carlo clapped his broad hands once. "I *knew* it! I was just thinking, I'll wager those are the nice girls from Verona. And sure enough!"

Alli had come back to stand at Franni's side. Carlo nodded at her courteously. "I just saw my dear old Bianca last week. She says you two didn't stay with her."

Franni and Alli exchanged an uncomfortable glance, but Carlo slapped his knee with a laugh. "Bianca's personality is not to everyone's taste. I'll grant you that."

Seeing the old man wasn't offended, Franni was eager to fill him in on their time in Mantua. "Alli's singing in the Duke's nephew's wedding, and I'm sewing costumes for the show!"

"*Franni*!" Alli warned. "No need to tell everybody everything."

Carlo beamed. "Well, well. I guess you landed on your feet. Climb aboard, and tell me all about it while I drive you to wherever you're staying."

Once again, Alli got to sit up front next to Carlo. But Franni's ride in back was much more comfortable this time, since there were no slabs of marble to squash in next to.

"I been here daily," said Carlo, "mainly bringing lumber for the new theater."

"That's where Alli's going to sing," said Franni, proud of her sister.

"Hush, Franni," Alli warned again. But she sounded rather proud of herself.

They told Carlo all about the production of *Arianna.* Franni also described the adventure with Luca pretending to be a duke. Alli didn't say much, but Franni made the story as colorful as possible. "And the guard pulled up his shirt to check in his birthmark. But it was all smudged from sweat."

"You don't say," Carlo said for the fiftieth time. He was driving them all the way around the Palazzo, the long way home, so Franni had a chance to finish the story.

"Oh, but it's true," Franni assured him. "Luca had painted the birthmark on. Right, Alli?" Alli nodded, staring silently at the Palazzo. Franni went ahead and told Carlo her theory about these strange events. "It's as if he pretended to be the Duke just so he could get people to like him. But he didn't want the authorities to catch him."

Carlo turned around and nodded sagely at her. "Can't blame him on that score. My philosophy is, whatever you're up to, keep the authorities out of it as much as you can."

Finally Alli spoke. "It was such a romantic idea, that a duke was hiding out among us. Every idiot in town got caught up in it." She turned back to catch Franni's eye. "Especially me."

Filled with pity, Franni tried to comfort her. "Hey, why couldn't it have been Luca? The real missing Duke must be out there somewhere. It was as likely he was in Mantua as anywhere else."

Alli smiled sadly. "Turns out he's 'anywhere else,' not in Mantua."

"Begging your pardon, miss," said Carlo to Alli, "but there's reason to believe that darn Duke really is in Mantua. Only nobody's found him yet."

Franni's heart raced. She pulled herself to her knees and leaned forward so she could hear everything Carlo said. Alli was flushed and wide-eyed. "Why do you say that?" she asked.

"You ever heard of an assassin named Pietro Fucilli?"

Alli shook her head. Franni, feeling woozy, slumped back down onto the hard wooden slats. She recognized the name. Edgardo had said it to her. But she didn't let on.

Carlo explained in a voice he might use to tell a ghost story. "He's a professional. He'll kill anyone for a price." Alli wrapped her shawl tighter around her shoulders. "And there's a rumor he's been spotted around these parts, ever since the announcement from Bergamo that they were looking for their Duke."

Franni pulled her knees to her chin and clenched her teeth.

Alli asked, "Why would someone want the Duke dead?"

"Someone who doesn't want his family to stay in power," said Carlo. "That Gritti family wants to take over ruling Bergamo, so they have to get rid of the last of his bloodline. They can't risk this fella being found before May the twenty-eighth." Franni tried to listen over the pounding of her heart. The memory of the assassin's awful face seemed to hang before her eyes in the dark.

But Alli didn't seem frightened. Just curious. "And people have seen this assassin? How can they be sure?"

Carlo pulled up to the curb in front of Maria's house. "Because," he said with gusto, "his eyes are crooked in his face. That's not a thing a man can hide."

To Franni's surprise, Alli laughed. "Oh, you're awful, Carlo. Such stories. Come on, Franni. Let's go inside."

"Didn't mean to scare you two," Carlo said as he helped them down from the cart.

"Don't be silly," said Alli. "We're not scared." She sighed, adding, "And there's no duke."

Franni saw the world around her like a blur. She waved distractedly as the tired, old horse dragged Carlo's wagon down the street. If Alli hadn't pulled her inside, she would have stayed out on the lawn all night.

They'd missed dinner, but Maria took pity on them and gave them a plate of dried dates. "These don't look like much," Maria said when Franni wrinkled her nose, "but they're delicious and nutritious. You can't always judge things by how they appear, you know."

Maria's words made Franni think about the story of the acorn. The little seed that became the giant tree, and the foolish man who turned out to be very—

All at once, something became clear to Franni, as clear as the full moon in the night sky over Mantua. She knew who the Duke of Bergamo was.

CHAPTER 17

THE NIGHT DRAGGED ON AND ON. All Franni could think about was Edgardo. Or the man she knew as Edgardo.

"Why are you pacing around?" Alli asked groggily. The moon was fat and its light poured through their bedroom window.

Franni felt that if she didn't tell someone what was on her mind, she would burst. Perching on the edge of Alli's bed, she whispered, "Edgardo."

"The little guy on the crew? What about him?"

"I think he's the missing duke."

Alli let loose a single whoop of laughter before pulling her blankets over her mouth. Then she whispered, obviously fighting back the giggles, "Franni, you're not serious, are you?"

Franni nodded slowly. Nobody wished more than she did that this was a joke.

"But that's ridiculous. He's a, he's a–" Alli buzzed her lips. "Well, he's not exactly tall with wavy brown hair, is he?"

Franni crossed her arms. "How would they know what he looks like? They have no idea."

"But the messenger from Bergamo said–"

"I was there when he announced his message." Franni's face felt hot. "He said only what they think the Duke *might* look like. He could actually look like *anything*."

But Alli wasn't buying it. "Franni, you're being silly." She lay back down on her pillow. "He's a *dwarf*, for goodness' sake. You really do let your imagination run away sometimes. Now, try to get some sleep. Tomorrow is the dress rehearsal, and it's going to be long and exhausting."

"Alli, wait. Just listen." But Alli rolled over toward the wall, pulling the blanket around her ears. Franni knew it was hopeless to try to convince her. All she could do was wait for the first light of day, when she could go out and find Edgardo.

As she lay there, the minutes crawling by, Franni mulled over every scrap of information she had about Edgardo and whether it was evidence for him being the Duke. The snippets of knowledge formed a list in her mind, and she considered each item carefully:

1. He's a dwarf. This is the biggest problem. Why wouldn't the monastery have known this?
2. He knows how to do lots of things. Maybe he's been on the run for a while, so he's worked at many different jobs. This could be because he ran away when he was young.
3. He knows about the assassin Pietro Fucilli. Edgardo was the first person to tell me who Fucilli is. And he looked pretty scared when I mentioned I'd seen him. Somebody who thought he was being chased would know about such things.
4. He seemed to believe right away that Luca was the Duke. Edgardo went out of his way to encourage me to believe it, too. But Luca himself was more interested in sharing that information with the young ladies in the chorus. None of the other men cared or noticed. Maybe Edgardo just wanted me to believe it so I wouldn't figure out the truth.
5. When the guards from Bergamo tried to search for the duke in the *Arianna* company, Edgardo knew just what to say to throw them off the scent. So he knows something about politics and nobility.

There was one more item on Franni's list. She was almost afraid to think about it. Sitting with her back to the wall, she pulled the blanket around her shoulders. It wasn't a cold night, but the memory she was picturing made her shudder:

6. Edgardo probably has a birthmark shaped like a fish. When he treated me so cruelly after he was injured, I thought he was behaving like a pet dog that turns on its master when it's hurt. Or that he was too proud to accept my help. But now I think he just didn't want me to see him with his shirt off. He was hiding his birthmark.

Franni sniffled and wiped tears from her face. Edgardo, who she thought was her closest friend, had lied to her. One of the biggest lies anyone had ever told her. She hated Mantua all over again, and she soaked poor Babbo in another flood of tears for her dead parents.

Why did we have to leave Verona? she asked Mama in Heaven. Then she pictured her stepfather, and asked a more pointed question. *Why did you have to marry that awful man?* Franni was old enough to know the answer. A widow with two daughters was very lucky to find any man willing to marry and support her. *Oh, but Mama,* she prayed into the dark, *he was so mean to us after the fever took you. It must have broken your heart to watch from up above.*

Her stepfather's scowling face seemed to grow bigger, made of moonlight and shadows. *He treated us like slaves, Mama. And he hit Alli. Oh, why couldn't he have been a kind man?*

The ghostly apparition changed to a face that calmed her, and Franni whispered to it. "Why couldn't he be like you, Edgardo?" She stared hard at the picture her mind had sketched. She realized that she didn't hate Edgardo. He was her friend no matter what, and she was afraid that something terrible might happen to him.

A gust of wind blew through the open window. The image before Franni's tear-filled eyes changed again and a third face appeared. It was broad and rough, with glowing eyes like pure evil. And one of those eyes was too low next to the nose. It was the horrid face of Pietro Fucilli. “Mama, Mama, please protect my friend Edgardo,” Franni prayed in a soft wail. “I’ve never had a big brother before, and I don’t know what I’d do if I lost him. And please, Mama, give me wisdom to know what to say to him tomorrow. Should I convince him to run away so he stays safe? But then I’d never see him again. Help me, Mama and Papa. I don’t know what to do.”

Franni fell asleep praying.

* * *

A pink line of sunshine played across Franni’s eyes, waking her. It was dawn. The cast and orchestra would gather at the new theater for final rehearsals in a few hours. But Franni knew the construction crew would get there much earlier. Probably they’d been working through the night to make sure the theater and sets were ready. It was the perfect opportunity to corner Edgardo and try to make him tell her the truth.

In the other bed, Alli was sleeping soundly, making a rhythmic whistling sound through her nose. While Franni hated to wake her sister, she also didn’t want her to worry. It was a tricky problem, almost as tricky as finding her petticoats and stockings in the dark room. Just as Franni was buttoning the front of her dress, she had a great idea.

From the bedside table she pulled the letter of appointment making Alli an official singer to Duke Gonzaga. As extravagant as the Duke was, the letter used only one side of the paper. Franni would use the other side. But she had no quill or ink. There were writing instruments in Maria’s room, since she needed them to keep track of the rent her tenants owed her. Still, Franni didn’t dare disturb Maria.

Then Franni remembered the kohl. Alli had “borrowed” the tiny pot of black eyeliner from the makeup tray during rehearsals one day. She loved how huge it made her eyes look. At the time, Franni had teased her for swiping it.

"What are you planning to do with that," she'd said, "walk around Mantua looking like a surprised raven?" But Alli had stuck out her tongue and slipped the soft black makeup into her bag.

If it will write on a person's face, Franni thought, *surely it will write on paper.* Pulling Alli's bag into the slash of pink sunlight, Franni dug around as quietly as she could. She found the pot wrapped in a scarf of wool fabric. Opening it, she ran the tip of her index finger over the black goop. She laid Alli's letter face down on the floor and wrote with her finger: "At new theater." She dipped her finger in the kohl again. "I'm right about Duke." Franni laid the paper next to Alli's head, but something bothered her.

She was still afraid Alli would think something was wrong, especially since they'd argued the night before. Franni needed a way to make the message seem lighthearted. And she had just the thing. Taking Babbo from under her own blanket, she propped him up against Alli's pillow and pinned the letter under his plush arms. *There, that's perfect.* Franni admired her little tableau.

But when she grabbed her shawl and stepped toward the door, her stomach knotted. What if this was goodbye? If she could figure out that Edgardo was the Duke, then so could Pietro Fucilli. Tomorrow, May 28, was the day the rival Gritti family would take over Bergamo. So Fucilli would strike today. He needed to eliminate any chance for the real Duke to come forward. Maybe Edgardo was already doomed. Maybe being at his side was the most dangerous place in Mantua. But Edgardo was her friend, and if there was a way to save him, she must try.

Franni clenched her teeth and fought the chill that gripped her. "Goodbye, Alli," she whispered. "Take care of Babbo." Closing her eyes, Franni crossed herself. "Watch over me, Mama and Papa." She took a deep breath and ran down the stairs and out of the house.

Franni was surprised by how many people were already on the streets. On any other morning she would have dawdled, watching the workers and peddlers and cleaners and groomsmen doing all their interesting tasks. But not today. Franni ran past them all, her footfalls echoing through the alleyways. A dog barked at her, maker her trot even faster. Finally she could see the gate around the St. George's Castle gardens. Somehow the familiar landmark made her aware of herself. So, so tired! A stitch in her side doubled Franni over, and she clutched at the edge of a marble fountain.

"Signorina, are you ill?" A man's voice came from behind Franni, and she twisted painfully to look up. It was a soldier, young and broad-shouldered. When Franni noticed his chiseled jaw and dark eyes, she automatically thought about how she wished Alli were there with her.

"I'm not sick, Signore," she panted, managing a weak curtsy. "I was just running."

He furrowed his black eyebrows. "And why were you running?"

The truth, Franni told herself. *A little truth is better than a big lie.* "I'm working on the entertainment for the wedding," she said.

The soldier's eyebrows shot upward. "*The* wedding?" He gestured around at all the garlands lining the streets. Franni nodded, but the man's eyebrows furrowed again. "Wait a minute. There are no entertainments today. His Highness took the wedding party to his other Palazzo, just outside the city." He folded his arms and frowned at Franni.

But she was ready with more truth. "Well, that's why today is so important. It's dress rehearsal."

"Of what, exactly?"

Exasperated, Franni almost shouted, "Maestro Monteverdi's musical tragedy, *Arianna.* The performance for his Serene Highness is tomorrow." She pointed down the street, past the castle gardens, toward the new theater. "I'm supposed to be *there* by now."

At last the soldier believed her. "You're in Maestro Monteverdi's show?"

Well, not exactly in it, thought Franni. But she nodded enthusiastically.

"Oh, that must be thrilling. Please, Signorina, allow me to escort you the rest of the way."

Well, well, well! Franni couldn't wait to tell her sister about this. The soldier had long legs, so Franni had to scurry to keep up. But it tickled her to see everyone else in the Via St. Georgio move out of the way to let them pass. For the first time, she sort of understood why Alli might want to be a Duchess. Even the sleepy guard in front of the theater snapped to attention when the soldier approached.

"She's here for *rehearsal,*" her escort announced dramatically. Franni got the feeling he'd really rather be onstage than defending the city. But she stopped herself from laughing, and thanked him with a few soldi coins.

"Papers?" said the theater guard. Franni flashed her gold-embossed letter quickly, hoping the soldier wouldn't notice she was only a seamstress. It was a huge relief when the guard yawned and waved her inside.

The maze-like corridors still reeked of sawdust and fresh paint. Very few torches burned along the walls. Franni assumed that was because of the risk of fire in the wooden building. But it certainly made it dark! She tried to grab a torch to carry with her, but they were mounted too high on the walls. All she could do was plod on ahead, trying to remember which turns would take her to the stage.

Eventually she heard men's voices, and she rounded the corner timidly. "Um, excuse me?"

Three men in the simple clothes of workmen stopped chatting and looked at her. One hailed her with a bottle of wine. "It's the sewing girl. Hello, sewing girl."

"Hello," Franni answered in a tiny voice.

The three men stepped forward. They stank of sweat and alcohol. "You want to measure us for costumes, my lovely?" asked the tallest one. He was bald, but his arms were hairy.

"Maybe she wants to learn how to dance so she can be in the show," said a skinny man with no front teeth. He put his hand out toward her. "Come here, sweetheart. Let me teach you to dance."

"Halt, you ugly, worthless knaves!" With a flood of relief, Franni recognized Edgardo's voice. But she couldn't see him. He kept up his threats. "Back away from

Signorina Ategnati, or I shall remove your entrails with this little toy."

The men did back away, grumbling and cursing. Once they'd moved, Franni could see Edgardo, and his "little toy" was not his usual bread knife. A long silver dagger glinted in the torchlight.

CHAPTER 18

ALTHOUGH HE CAME UP ONLY to their waists, Edgardo clearly scared the three men. It wasn't just how sharp the blade looked, Franni decided. It was Edgardo's bearing as he wielded the dagger. He looked like he had natural power and strength far beyond his size. Now, more than ever, Franni felt sure she was right about him.

Once the men had scampered off like rats, Edgardo gave Franni a quizzical look. "What are you doing here, Snailnose? Costumes won't be needed for at least two hours."

Franni could see no point in delaying, so she plunged right on in. "You're the Duke of Bergamo." It came out harshly, as if she were accusing him of some awful crime. In a much gentler voice, she added, "Aren't you?"

Edgardo's face barely changed. But Franni detected the tiniest wince, like he'd make if he had a nail in his shoe but was determined to walk normally. Franni continued. "You have the birthmark on your back."

Edgardo grinned. "Nonsense. You've never seen a mark on my back."

Hearing him still deny the truth made Franni's stomach knot. That wasn't how a friend behaved! "You threw me out when I tried to help you." She swallowed down a sob, refusing to cry. "I was so worried when you got cut, but you chased me out like a dog. You just didn't want me to see your birthmark."

Edgardo fidgeted, shifting his weight and staring at the floor. Franni went on. "You don't fool me. The guards from Bergamo may have missed you. The bounty hunters may have gotten it wrong. But I don't give up so easily." She took a step closer to Edgardo, making him look up. "And neither does Pietro Fucilli."

Running his fingers through his hair, Edgardo sounded agitated. "I can't talk about this, Franni. It would put you in danger."

Franni shook her head. "Don't you understand? It's too late to keep pretending. Tomorrow's the deadline to claim the dukedom, so Fucilli's going to kill you today." She bent slightly and repeated that word right into his face. "*Today.*"

"Franni, you should go home." Edgardo put his hands out. "I'll leave Mantua, okay?"

Exasperated, Franni shook her head. "Edgardo, you don't have to run. Why won't you just be the Duke?"

"What?"

"Tell the Duke of Mantua who you really are," Franni reasoned. "His guards will protect you."

Edgardo chewed his lip for a minute before saying, "But then I'd have to–" He stopped, looking up at Franni with pleading eyes.

Franni felt sorry for him. She nodded. "Yes, you'd have to go to Bergamo and be the Duke. But, Edgardo, it's what you were born to be." He squinted, making a doubtful face. But Franni was sure of what she was saying. "Think about it. Your mother's family tried to hide you away. They didn't want you to know what you were. But you knew you didn't belong at that monastery."

"That's for sure." Edgardo motioned for Franni to follow him down a narrow hallway. "Let's find a better place to talk."

Edgardo led Franni into an empty dressing room lined with tables and chairs. He pulled out a chair for Franni and climbed up onto the one next to it. Then he rubbed his eyes with the heels of his hands. "Honestly, I never thought it would come to this."

"What do you mean?"

"I didn't think my bloodline would ever matter. I thought the Duke and Duchess would have plenty of children, and they'd just forget about me."

"But they didn't forget."

Edgardo gave a hollow laugh. "No, and I bet they gave that monastery plenty of money to keep me." His laugh turned gleeful. "And I'll also bet they were plenty annoyed when they found out, twenty years later, that the monks hadn't raised me after all!"

Franni remembered list of evidence she'd come up with the night before. She took a big breath and tried to ask an embarrassing question. "Why didn't the monks tell the Bergamo guards that you were, um–"

Edgardo smiled. "A dwarf? Ha! I bet they didn't know. Last time they saw me, I was probably just rather short for a little kid. How were they to guess I'd never get any taller?"

Franni had to snicker at that.

"They were cruel to me, most of the monks," Edgardo said, suddenly serious. "One of the kind ones, Father Tomaso, took me away one night."

"How old were you?"

"About five, I guess."

"But you knew about being the Duke's son?"

Edgardo nodded. "Father Tomaso told me about my bloodline. And the birthmark. He brought me to a farmer's family, near Manzo."

"So, that was the truth!" Franni exclaimed.

"Yes, Snailnose," smiled Edgardo. "I told you as much of the truth as I dared. I never wanted to deceive you. Anyway, my new family, the Ruggieri, did their best to raise me." Sighing, he stared into the distance. "They were good people. I was just–restless."

The sad look on Edgardo's face made Franni's heart ache. "You know what my papa used to say?" She could hear her father speaking these words as she said them, and her voice cracked. "The good Lord will tell you when you've found where you belong." She leaned toward her friend. "You've been all over the place. You've tried everything. Maybe it's because you haven't found your place. I think you're supposed to be the Duke."

Running his finger over a scratch in the wooden table, Edgardo spoke glumly. "But I wouldn't be free anymore." He looked up with a changed expression. "Hey, maybe I could just hide out for a couple of days, and the Gritti family will take over Bergamo, and I'll be safe. Fucilli will have no reason to kill me then."

Franni said nothing, but stared at her hands. Disappointment made her bones feel like lead. Finally she found the energy to speak. "If you hide out while your enemies take over your city, innocent people will get killed. And everybody says the Gritti family will treat people badly if they rule the city. If you let that happen, you won't be my friend anymore." Without looking at Edgardo, she walked out of the room.

Franni thought she would spend a little while in the castle gardens next door. It would soothe her nerves before the long day of rehearsal. The problem was, she couldn't remember which way to turn in the maze of backstage hallways. She took one corner after another, but she never seemed to be closer to the exit.

She passed a few workers, groggy men who pointed and grunted when she asked for directions. At least they weren't awful to her, like that threesome earlier. But they weren't very helpful, either. Eventually she came upon a tall man, kneeling over to fix the buckle on his boot. Franni figured it was worth one more try.

Running up to him, she said, "Excuse me, Signore. I wonder if you could please tell me which way—"

The man looked up and Franni's body turned to ice. His eyes were crooked. It was Pietro Fucilli. She'd never been so close to him. He was tall. He could step on Edgardo like an insect. And then she blinked and he was gone, slipped into the shadows.

Franni took two shaking breaths, thinking furiously. Sure, she'd love to escape. But she had to warn Edgardo that Fucilli was there. So she turned around and ran toward what she prayed was the direction of the stage.

Her heart was beating so fast, she could barely run. The air seemed to press back on her, as if she were underwater. Somehow she made it around two corners.

She tried to picture Edgardo's face, to give her hope and a reason to move. It worked. Franni ran. She ran like Fucilli was after *her*, her skirts swooshing past the workers and props in the hallway. Another turn in the hallway. She could hear the sounds of workmen on the stage. Franni started to shout. "Edgardo! Edgardo! Edgardo Ruggiero! He's here! Get out, Edgardo!"

She didn't know whether he was nearby, but she kept on shouting. Practically screaming. Surely he could hear her, wherever he was. And then there was an awful sound behind her. The click of boot buckles, each one seeming a little closer to Franni. "Edgardo!" she screeched. Right turn. She glanced back and there was Fucilli, lurching down the corridor. He tripped on a prop tree someone had carelessly laid on its side. Franni didn't stick around to find out if he got up again.

Rounding the corner, she could see the backstage area. "Edgardo!"

"I'm here, Franni." Her friend was standing on the stage, a pulley wheel in his hands.

"Fucilli!" she wailed, but her warning was too late. The assassin had nearly caught up.

Edgardo seemed calm. "Make certain it's raining out today," he said.

Franni was baffled. All she could think about was Fucilli's heavy breathing. He ran right past her onto the stage, and Franni covered her eyes. She couldn't bear to see what would happen to Edgardo. Expecting to hear Egardo cry out in pain, instead she heard Fucilli growling, "Where is he? Where's the half-man?"

Franni looked up and peered out onto the stage. There was no sign of Edgardo. But where could he have gone? He wasn't behind the canvas backdrop. Fucilli made sure of that by slicing through it with his dagger. The only props onstage were the wave corkscrew, a large rock, and the mechanical cloud.

"Oh!" The sound burst from Franni's mouth when she recalled what Edgardo had said. "Make certain it's raining out today." He was hiding in the cloud! Fucilli was thrashing around the wings, overturning every prop he could find, and terrifying the crew. Franni watched him examine pulley-operated ship just offstage. Any moment he would come back the other direction and notice that the cloud was hollow.

Franni grabbed the ladder and climbed. No monkey ever climbed faster. She kept climbing even when her foot caught in her petticoat and she ripped it down the seam. As she reached the top platform, she grabbed the crank and pushed with all her strength. It barely budged. "Help!" she cried.

Someone was coming up the ladder behind her. What if it was Fucilli? She would be trapped up there. Some ropes hung near her from the ceiling. She tried to picture grabbing one and swinging to safety, but it was a ridiculous idea. She was no pirate! She'd never swung from a rope in her life.

Franni searched the platform for something to hit Fucilli in the head with, but nothing was loose. *I can kick him*, she thought.

Up popped Natalia's head. "Can I help you, dear?"

There was no one Franni less expected to see. She was too stunned to move. Natalia climbed up next to her in a most unladylike fashion. "Don't just stand there. Let's crank!" ordered the head seamstress. So Franni pushed and Natalia pulled. The crank moved half a rotation. "Faster," hissed Franni. She pulled and Natalia pushed, another half turn. And around and around they went. Franni's arm burned, but a quick peek over the side told her the cloud was rising.

"Your sister . . . told Maria . . . you were . . . here," Natalia panted. "Knew something . . . was wrong . . . I always liked . . . little Edgardo."

Now the cloud was so high that Edgardo could wave at Franni.

"Come down here!" roared Fucilli, shaking his fist. "You come down or else I'll come up, and it won't end well for that little girl."

Fucilli took a step toward the ladder.

CHAPTER 19

"HEY, SNAILNOSE," EDGARDO called from the cloud. "Looks like rain right about now, wouldn't you say?"

Before Franni could answer, Edgardo jumped off the cloud, his dagger clutched in his right hand. Natalia screamed as he landed on Fucilli's shoulders, toppling him. In seconds, the stage was crowded with crew members, suddenly full of courage now that the dangerous man was flat on his face. They held Fucilli down and bound his hands and feet.

"Make way!" came a voice from the back row in the huge theater. "Make way for the Palazzo Guard!"

"I told your sister to call for them," said Natalia as they watched the guards swarm toward the stage. "She was very worried about you." Franni smiled at the thought that the Palazzo Guard was there, not for the Duke of Bergamo, but to save *her*. A handsome soldier helped her down the ladder, and she could hardly resist the urge to tell him what a nice, pretty sister she had.

But then she noticed Edgardo. He was leaning against the mechanical waves, looking sour.

"All hail the Duke," said Franni. But it was the tiniest peep of sound, and everyone ignored her. She spoke up. "All hail his most Serene Highness, the Duke of Bergamo!"

That made everyone stop and bow their heads, even the guards. Franni couldn't resist a quick glance up at Edgardo's face. His mouth was crumpled into a frown. But as soon as he noticed Franni, he smiled. And he bowed to *her*!

Pietro Fucilli was dragged away, struggling and cursing. But the two guards with the fanciest gold armor stayed behind and knelt before Edgardo. This made them about the same height as the standing dwarf, Franni noticed. Edgardo took a step back, as he might from a pile of horse droppings on the street. "What do you fellows want?"

The guards glanced at each other, and one of them spoke. "If Your Highness will forgive us, we must humbly request proof of your identity." The guard swallowed hard, as if he expected to be struck.

Edgardo's face brightened. "Oh! Well, then, I'm sorry to disappoint you lads, but I have no proof. I am nobody." He crossed his arms over his puffed-up chest, looking very smug.

Franni wasn't going to stand for that nonsense. "He has the birthmark," she told the guards. "Just check his back."

The guards stood, looking very uncomfortable. If Edgardo really was the Duke, they would get in a lot of trouble for forcing him to lift his tunic. Franni could see that Edgardo was enjoying the awkward situation far too much. She walked right up to him and wagged her finger as she told him off. "Show them the birthmark, 'Your Serene Highness,' or you're not going to be feeling so serene!"

Many people gasped—it was unthinkable to address a duke that way—but Edgardo burst out laughing. "Why, I should put you in shackles and make you scrub the floors with your tongue."

Franni didn't even blink. "You can't do any of that if you don't prove you're the Duke."

Smirking, Edgardo addressed the guards in a theatrical whisper, jerking his thumb toward Franni. "The problem with *that* one is, she's too smart for her own good." He heaved a deep sigh and rolled his eyes. "Very well. I suppose I must admit that I am, in fact, Marco Coriglio D'Espelina, the Second, true heir to the blasted Dukedom of Bergamo in the Republic of Venice." He sighed again.

"And, if all the females present would kindly turn around, I shall show you the proof you seek."

He made a twirling motion with his finger. Franni, Natalia, plus all the other women who'd been gathering on the stage, turned their backs. The men of the crew and cast, on the other hand, drew in closer. Even some of the orchestra players pushed past Franni, clutching their instruments.

"Let me see," said a familiar voice. Franni took a quick peek, and was amused to see Maestro Monteverdi himself striding toward the guards.

"Don't crowd me," Edgardo commanded. "And, Franni, no peeking."

She turned her head, wishing she would have a chance to see the sign of her friend's destiny. But then, she knew in her heart he was the Duke. She didn't need the birthmark to prove it.

"Oh, look at that," someone said.

Another man said, "It really does look like a fish, swimming toward his spine."

It was all Franni could do not to steal a glance at that fish! She heard a rustling around her, and turned just enough to see all the men bending on one knee.

"Oh!" said Iulia, who was standing nearby. She curtsied. "Your Highness."

Natalia curtsied. Georgia curtsied. After searching the crowd, Franni finally spied Alli, who was curtsying so low her legs seemed to sink into the stage under her skirts.

A guard pointed menacingly at Franni. "You! Show your respect to the Duke of Bergamo!"

Embarrassed, Franni muttered, "Oh, yes, sorry," and bent her knees and bowed her head. But she couldn't help smiling. Her own friend Edgardo was a real, live duke! Franni vowed never to stop reminding Alli of this fact.

With military precision, the two gold-armored guards escorted the new duke out of the theater. Franni felt a lump in her throat as she watched him go, swinging his little arms to keep up with the guards' long strides. *I'll never see him again,* she thought. But she chased her sorrow away with a happier realization. *He's my friend. I just know he'll come and say goodbye before he leaves.*

Franni didn't have a lot of time to worry about missing Edgardo. The director Striggio clapped his hands and announced the start of rehearsals. Natalia called the costume and makeup crew back to the dressing rooms and gave them all kinds of instructions. Franni thought her head would burst from trying to remember who changed into which costume when. And then there was the challenge of learning where she should stand during each scene. She was expected to be in the right place to unhook buttons, hand Theseus his cloak, help drape the tapestry of Dionysus's throne, and a hundred other tasks.

After lunch they ran through the whole thing with the singers. It was a disaster. Three costumes got ripped when singers changed too fast or caught capes or skirts on the scenery. Signore Rinuccini was furious when Rasi, the tenor playing Theseus, forgot the words to his aria three times. Maestro Monteverdi insulted Caccini's women from Florence by claiming they sounded flat. They threatened to send for a coach back to Florence immediately.

The crew had just as many problems as the cast. When Franni accidentally brought Madame Andreini the blue Arianna dress rather than the ivory one, Natalia said she'd hang Franni by her ears. And, of course, the crank mechanism for the waves got jammed and the rope to pull the ship across the stage had a knot in it, so the ship foundered at sea.

Simply a disaster, everyone agreed.

But after supper, which was catered to the theater, everything changed. The singers sang beautifully. The orchestra didn't miss a beat. The correct props and costumes showed up at the right times and places. It was all very professional. Franni could see on everyone's exhausted faces just what she was feeling: Maybe tomorrow they would put on an entertainment they could be proud of.

Oh, Franni was tired! She, Alli, Iulia, and Georgia dragged themselves home together, walking two by two through the alleyways to Maria's house. None of them said a word. Not even a street singer, lilting a beautiful ballad and playing a lute, could interest Franni. All she could think about was bed. Feather pillow. Blankets. Sweet, sweet sleep.

The women at Maria's not involved in *Arianna* swarmed around when Franni and her friends walked in the door. "Is that dwarf really the Duke?" they asked. "Did they really arrest that scary assassin?" and a hundred more questions. But Franni and Alli waved them away.

The stairs to their bedroom seemed steeper than the side of Mount Aetna. Franni was even too tired to pick Babbo off the floor by Alli's bed and place him on her own pillow. Alli groaned, sounding as achy as Franni felt, struggling to undo the buttons and ties of her dress. But Franni didn't even bother to take off her clothes. She fell face down onto the wonderfully soft world of slumber.

* * *

It was an annoying sound, and Franni wished it would stop. She snuggled deeper into the blankets and clamped her pillow over her head. But somebody yanked the pillow right out from under her arm. Now she could hear that the annoying sound was Maria's voice.

"Get up. Get up, Franni."

Franni tried to ask, "Is it morning?" but her tongue was still sleeping.

"Get up right now, Franni." Maria poked her hard in the shoulder blade. "Right now. Don't dawdle."

Franni lifted her head. An emergency? She finally understood. "Alli okay?" she asked automatically.

"I'm fine, Franni, but you have to go to the Palazzo."

Very confused, Franni sat up. "Not the Palazzo," she said. "The performance is at the new theater." She rubbed her eyes, wishing everyone would let her sleep.

Alli came and sat next to her on the mattress. "Franni, it's the middle of the night. You've been called to the Palazzo. The Duke wants to see you."

Franni perked up at the news. "Edgardo wants to see me?"

But Maria laughed. “No, dear. The Duke of Mantua.”

Trying to comprehend, Franni squinted and cocked her head. “That’s silly. The Duke of Mantua is in the middle of the wedding festivities. Why would he want to see me? I’m just an assistant seamstress.”

Maria shrugged. “It’s not our place to ask such questions. All I know is, there are two Palazzo guards standing in my front hallway, waiting for you. So, let’s get you ready to meet the Duke.”

Half stunned and half asleep, Franni didn’t resist when Maria and Alli helped her into a clean dress and combed her hair. They practically carried her down the stairs like a rag doll. As promised, there were the two guards in the font hallway. They bowed. They actually bowed at Franni, and each offered her an elbow to help her walk. By now, all the residents in Maria’s boarding house were up and peering around corners and through banisters.

“Good luck, Franni,” Iulia called.

One of the guards had opened the door when Alli ran up and put both her hands on Franni’s face. “Curtsy. Don’t look directly at him. Be respectful. Agree to any work he offers you. Tell him anything he wants to know.”

Despite the butterflies doing acrobatics in her chest, Franni didn’t feel like being babied. “Okay, *okay*. Don’t worry. I won’t embarrass you.” Without waiting for the guards, she marched out the door. The gold paint decorating the coach glimmered in the torch light. Franni felt herself lifted up and lowered onto the softest velvet seat she’d ever known. It was softer than a puppy’s belly. The horse pulled so smoothly, Franni might have been riding in a boat on a calm lake. Franni smiled out the window. Now, *this* was the way to travel!

Within minutes they’d arrived, pulling into the courtyard of the the Palazzo Ducale. And not to the servants’ wing, but to the main entrance! A whole flank of palace guards in shimmering armor stood tall when she passed by. Franni began to think this wasn’t real. She must still be face-down on her bed at Maria’s.

But the dream didn’t stop. Two liverymen in long peach-colored coats pulled open the double doors of the palace. Franni stepped into a paradise of polished marble paintings, silver, and gold.

“Miss Francesca Ategnati,” announced another well-dress servant. Bowing, he swept his arm toward two people at the other end of the room. “Their Most Serene Highnesses, the Dukes of Mantua and of Bergamo.”

CHAPTER 20

FRANNI TORE HER EYES AWAY from the painting of a shepherdess on the ceiling, and there stood Duke Gonzaga. Next to him, to her amazement, was Edgardo.

"You should be in Bergamo!" she shouted. "The Gritti family will take over the city if they don't know you've been found!"

The two dukes had slight smiles on their faces. Mortified by how she'd behaved, Franni heard Alli's words echoing in her mind. "Curtsy. Don't look directly at him." Too late, Franni bowed her head and saw the expensive embroidered shoes of the Duke of Mantua step toward her.

"Rise, my child." A chuckle escaped through his words.

She straightened, but kept her eyes down. "Your Highness?"

"Your concern for Duke D'Espelina and his fair city does you credit. We have sent a messenger to Bergamo with a ducal letter, so you needn't worry about that."

Franni wasn't sure what to say. Her heart fluttered with relief. "Thank you, Your Highness." She longed to look up and smile at Edgardo, but she didn't dare.

"I realize it's late, Signorina Ategnati," Duke Gonzaga continued. "We're all tired. However, I wish to thank you personally for your good deeds. Not only did you save Duke D'Espelina here, but you also helped catch one of the most dangerous men in Italy."

Surprised, Franni looked up, although she knew she wasn't supposed to.

"That's right," said the Duke. "My men have been trying to apprehend Pietro Fucilli for years, but with no luck. It never occurred to me to hire a twelve-year-old girl for the job. A serious oversight on my part. Merulo?" He gestured at a servant, who bowed and handed the Duke and opened wooden box. From it, the Duke pulled a gold chain with a large gold pendant. "A medal for bravery, my dear."

As Franni curtsied, she felt her knees shake.

"Your Highness," said the Duke of Mantua, "please do the honors."

Franni glanced up to meet Edgardo's smile after he stepped forward. She had to bow very low so he could reach around her neck to drape the heavy chain over it. Franni tried not to show her discomfort. She was determined to make Alli proud, not to mention her parents watching from above.

"You deserve it," said Edgardo, or rather, Duke D'Espelina. "And now I must ask you, Francesca Ategnati, if you would honor the city of Bergamo by coming to live there."

Franni scrunched up her nose, not sure if the offer was a joke. Or even a threat, considering she'd forced Edgardo to become the duke. "What would I have to do there?" she asked. "Would you make me scrub the floor with my tongue?"

"*What?*" the Duke of Mantua demanded to know.

But the Duke of Bergamo put his head back and laughed. "My dear Snailnose, you may do whatever you like in Bergamo. Or nothing at all. What do you think?"

Franni studied the different types of marble fitted together on the floor. She had been so sure that she wanted to leave Mantua. But now that she had that opportunity, Mantua seemed like home. And there was Alli to consider. The city of Bergamo probably didn't have its own Maestro Monteverdi for her to work with.

"Franni?" Edgardo whistled and waved his hand in front of her face. "Are you in there?"

She focused her eyes and looked up, feeling guilty. "Um, your Serene Highness?" she said. Calling Edgardo felt awkward. "Do I have to go to Bergamo?"

Duke Gonzaga spoke up. "Let me answer that. Signorina Ategnati, you are most welcome to stay in Mantua. In fact, we'll find you comfortable quarters in the Palazzo."

Franni curtsied for the hundredth time, trying to decide what to say. "Thank you, Your Highness." She swallowed, getting up the nerve for what she needed to ask. "And if I stay in Mantua, do I have to keep on being a seamstress?"

Hearing Edgardo snicker, she shot him a glance not at all appropriate for a Duke.

"You do not wish to be a seamstress?" Duke Gonzaga seemed surprised when she shook her head. "Hmm. And what is it you would prefer, my dear?"

Franni didn't answer at first, embarrassed to say what was in her heart. But Edgardo smiled kindly. "Tell him the truth, Snailnose."

She cleared her throat. "I'd like to learn to work on sets. Design them or paint them, or build the pulleys that move the clouds around."

Edgardo was beaming. "Extraordinary, isn't she?"

"Indeed," agreed Duke Gonzaga, "but that's a lot of professions to learn all at once." He scratched his chin. "I'll tell you what I'll do. Recently I brought a Flemish fellow, Peter Paul Rubens, to live in Mantua and paint for me."

"He does very nice work," Edgardo nodded.

"Perhaps, Signorina, I could persuade him to teach you a bit about colors and forms and perspective. Just to get you started, eh?"

"A capital idea, Your Highness!" Edgardo exclaimed.

"So glad you approve, Your Highness." The taller duke leaned down to shake the shorter one's hand.

Franni, feeling excited and confident, decided to risk asking for another favor. "And my sister, Alessandra? May she stay and sing for Maestro Monteverdi?"

Duke Gonzaga got a pained expression on his face. "I'll confide a secret to you, my dear. Maestro Monteverdi is a prickly character. And, in general, I find that he does what he wants. But I shall strongly encourage him to retain Alessandra in his company."

"Oh, thank you, thank you, Your Highness!" Without thinking, Franni grabbed the Duke's right hand and kissed it. Three guards pulled their swords halfway out of their scabbards. Franni froze at the scraping of metal on metal.

"You're not supposed to touch him," said Edgardo as Duke Gonzaga held up his hands to stop his guards.

"Never mind," said the Duke of Mantua. "It's settled, then. You and your sister will stay here. And, let's see. There was one more thing." He turned to his servant. "Merulo? What am I forgetting, blast it all?"

"*Arianna*, Your Highness."

"Ah, yes." Gonzaga shook his head. "Silly me. Sometimes, I forget my own name." He addressed Franni earnestly. "This new Duke of Begamo," he indicated Edgardo, "being in my glorious city during these blessed wedding festivities, must attend the performance of *Arianna* tomorrow as my guest."

"Oh, but he has to operate the cloud!" Franni blurted out.

Edgardo laughed so hard at that, a tear fell down his cheek. "My priceless Snailnose!"

But the Duke of Mantua looked baffled. "Yes, well, I don't think we can allow nobility to climb around on the scenery, eh? Heaven knows, I'm paying a big enough crew. Surely someone else can, er, operate the cloud."

At an angle so Duke Gonzaga couldn't see, Edgardo made a sour face and crossed his eyes. Franni bit the inside of her cheeks to keep from laughing.

"As I was saying," continued the Duke of Mantua with a suspicious glance next to him at Edgardo, "Duke D'Espelina needs a companion to escort to *Arianna*. Seeing as you saved his life, I thought it proper to invite you, Signorina Ategnati."

Franni had several reactions at once, and they all came pouring out. "That would be just so magical! Oh, my sister will be so jealous. And what will Signora Natalia do without me to help with costume changes? Oh, my goodness, what in the world would I wear?"

Edgardo grinned with delight. Duke Gonzaga looked wide-eyed and pale, like someone who'd been attacked by a hundred rabbits that came out of nowhere, hopped all over him, and left suddenly.

The servant Merulo stepped forward. "If you'll permit me, Signorina, I can help. Natalia Benotti is currently in the theatrical sewing room, preparing a gown for this very purpose. It will be ready by tomorrow. I trust that will be satisfactory?"

Franni stared at Merulo, speechless.

"Well, then," said the Duke of Mantua with obvious relief. "That's that, taken care of. Someone will take you home, Signorina. My thanks, again." He nodded stiffly, spun around, and walked from the room, guards on either side.

Franni curtsied deeply although he was walking away from her. When she rose and turned to Edgardo, her eyes were full of tears.

"See you tomorrow, Franni," he said quietly. "We'll have fun." He gave a perfect courtly bow, one leg forward, one arm back, as if he'd been doing it all his life.

* * *

Wednesday, May 28, 1608

A coach must have driven her home, and somehow she'd entered Maria's house and gone up the stairs to their bedroom. For all Franni knew, she'd floated all the way from the Palazzo. She sat up the rest of the night, waiting for the sun to rise. When Alli woke up, Franni told her what had happened. Once she'd showed off her gold medal, she started with the news she thought would please Alli the most.

"We can stay in Mantua, and we'll have quarters in the Palazzo."

Alli pressed both her hands against her mouth, as if she were trying to hold in a scream. A faint squeaking sound escaped from between her fingers.

Slightly worried that she might overexcite her sister, Franni continued. “You can keep singing for the Maestro, and I’m getting painting lessons.”

Alli’s hands moved to her heart. “Oh, Franni, that’s wonderful!”

The last piece of news was the most difficult to tell. Franni couldn’t look Alli in the eye when she said, “I’m supposed to attend the performance of *Arianna* with Edgar— I mean, with Duke D’Espalino.”

Sheepishly, she checked Alli’s face for anger or jealousy. But she found delight there instead. “You’ll be able to watch me!” Alli gushed. “You can tell me what we look like and sound like from the audience. Oh, and you must promise to notice what all the noble ladies are wearing. And look for handsome young men who don’t seem to be married, but who enjoy the music. And, if you get a chance, you might say, ‘That’s my sister’ when I sing my little solo in Act II.”

Franni beamed and took Alli’s hand. “Believe me, I won’t be able to stop bragging.” Leaning forward, she gave Alli a hug. “Have a wonderful show. I can’t wait to see it! Mama and Papa must be so proud of you.” When she pulled back, they were both sniffling.

“They’re proud of you, too, my darling Franni,” said Alli. “I just know it.”

* * *

At ten o’clock in the morning a ducal coach came to fetch Franni. Most of the women in *Arianna* had already left for the theater, so it was up to Maria to lecture her on behavior and bundle her off. The streets of Mantua were bathed in sunlight and strewn with wedding flowers. When the coach arrived at the Palazzo, Franni noticed that even the guards had shiny new uniforms.

It felt like dreaming again, walking through the marble hallways to the sewing room. For the first time, instead of slinking in so her lateness wasn’t noticed, Franni was heralded with an official announcement. “Signorina Francesca Ategnati!”

Natalia had deep rings around her eyes, but she was smiling. “Try this on, Franni,” she said, and held up a sky-blue silk dress with lace panels around the bodice. The waistline was decorated with green jewels. “They’re real emeralds,” said Donata, who hobbled forward holding a small box. “And you’re to wear this choker.” It was also emeralds, set in silver. Franni had no words as they dressed her, fixed her hair, and took her out for Merulo to escort to the waiting coach.

In the coach was another surprise. It was Edgardo, looking every inch a duke in his jacket of deep blue velvet striped with ivory silk.

“Oh!” exclaimed Franni when she saw him.

“Oh, yourself,” joked Edgardo. “I’ll venture to say that, of the six thousand guests present today, we two will be the prettiest.”

Six thousand! Franni had forgotten how many people would be there. But as soon as they arrived at the theater, there was so much to look at that she forgot to be nervous. Each dress was more beautiful than the last. Each tiara more expensive and sparkly. Each plate of food more delicous. Franni ate five of them.

After she and Edgardo were led to their seats, Franni suddenly realized something awful. She turned to Edgardo, the new Duke of Bergamo. “Will I ever see you again?”

His grin lifted her spirits immediately. “Why, of course, silly. I’ll visit you. You’ll visit me. And someday, if you’re a true friend, I’ll teach you my secret for making a cloud fly up and down.” Franni believed him.

Some servants tapped sticks on the floor, and the wealthiest audience in Italy turned its attention to the stage. As the instruments began to play from behind the scenes, Franni was thrilled to see the cloud sinking downward, right on cue.

“Oh, please, oh, please,” whispered Edgardo. But he needn’t have worried. It floated down smoothly, and a robed woman playing Tragedy stepped off to introduce the story.

The orchestra’s playing was as perfectly as the movements of the cloud, the waves, and the ship. Even the high-strung theorbo player sounded steady. Franni knew

Maestro had been ruthless and mean to the musicians, but now she knew why. They made a gorgeous harmony.

"Just lovely," whispered a woman in front of her, turning her hat when she spoke so that Franni had trouble seeing the stage.

When she first noticed Alli onstage, Franni gripped Edgardo's arm so tightly he had to pry her fingers loose. Alli, face painted a beautiful white, dressed in a shimmering blue gown that Franni had hemmed herself. Alli Ategnati, singing for the Duke of Mantua and his six thousand closest friends! Franni was sure she could hear her sister's voice above all the other women in the chorus.

The waves rolled smoothly. Frannie and Edgardo exchanged an approving nod. And the ship, with Theseus in it, rolled across the stage on its invisible rope.

"Why, it looks just like the sea!" exclaimed an elderly man a few rows ahead of Franni. Edgardo waggled his eyebrows at that compliment.

Playing the role of Arianna, Madame Andreini made the greatest impression on everyone. Nobody would have guessed that she had learned her part in only two weeks. Looking lost and disheveled, she began to sing the lament Maestro Monteverdi had written just for her. She sang about how she wished to die, and the audience sighed in sympathy.

Franni noticed that she didn't have the sweetest voice, but it was so expressive that Franni felt every ounce of Arianna's anguish in her own chest.

"Oh, my Theseus," sang the heartbroken Arianna, "yes, I still call you mine even though you left me."

Franni struggled to keep a sob from bursting out of her throat.

"Although I've been scorned, the fire of love is not put out."

In the corner of her eye, Franni saw Edgardo wipe his face with a handkerchief.

"This is the fate for a woman who loves too much and trusts too much."

The music came to a mournful end. At first, the only sounds in the theater were sobs. Franni was sure she had never been so sad. But then the crowd rose, all six thousand souls, and shook the building's new beams with applause and cheers.

Franni cheered, too. She cheered for life and music, dukes and palaces, sisters and friends. And, more than anything else, she cheered for Mantua, her new home.

ABOUT THE AUTHOR

ANNE E. JOHNSON TAUGHT MUSIC history for many years in New York City, specializing in the Baroque and Renaissance periods, and she feels a particular connection to the music and times of Claudio Monteverdi. Besides fiction, she has also written performing arts journalism for publications including *The New York Times* and *Stagebill Magazine.* Dozens of her short stories, for both kids and adults, have appeared in print and online.

Anne lives in Brooklyn with her husband, playwright Ken Munch. When she's not writing or editing, she's probably baking or going to concerts and plays. Her website is http://AnneEJohnson.com.

www.ingramcontent.com/pod-product-compliance
Lightning Source LLC
Chambersburg PA
CBHW031623040426
42452CB00007B/649

* 9 7 8 1 6 2 0 0 6 7 0 3 1 *